MW00604242

TAMING YOUR
DRAGONS

Making Peace with Your Emotions

SUE-ANNE MACGREGOR
and DAVID BARNES

PEACE of **MIND**
PARTNERS

TAMING YOUR DRAGONS

Making Peace with Your Emotions

Sue-Anne MacGregor and David Barnes

Published by Peace of Mind Partners.

Cover design and interior layout by Amy W. Evans. All rights reserved.
Cover photo ©iStockphoto.com/William Sherman

PEACE OF MIND
PARTNERS

Editing by Claudia Volkman of Creative Editorial Solutions.

Cartoon on page 42 © Arnie Levin, The New Yorker Collection, www.cartoonbank.com.
Cartoon on page 214 © Lee Lorenz, The New Yorker Collection, www.cartoonbank.com.

Library of Congress Control Number: 2013906945

ISBN 978-0-9892873-0-2

PRINTED IN THE UNITED STATES OF AMERICA

FIRST EDITION

Disclaimer: This publication contains our opinions and the ideas that have worked for us.
It is intended to provide helpful and informative material on understanding your emotions
and finding your own way. The authors of this book do not dispense medical advice or
prescribe the use of any technique as a form of treatment for physical, emotional, or medical
problems without the advice of a physician, either directly or indirectly. The intent of
the authors is only to offer information of a general nature to help you in your quest for
emotional and spiritual well-being. In the event that you use any of the information in this
book for yourself, which is your constitutional right, the authors and publisher assume no
responsibility for your actions.

dedication

We dedicate this book to all our teachers
and thank them for their wisdom.

TABLE OF CONTENTS

CHAPTER 3:
YOUR ENERGETIC SYSTEM
IS YOUR EMOTIONAL SYSTEM . . . . PAGE 55

CHAPTER 4:
THIS IS PERFECT – HOW DO I KNOW?
BECAUSE IT'S HAPPENING! . . . . PAGE 87

CHAPTER 5:
THE FEATHER OR THE TWO-BY-FOUR:
YOU CHOOSE. . . . . PAGE 117

TAMING YOUR DRAGONS

PREFACE

Intentions for This Book

❖ Gain insight into your emotional side and how you can make use of it

❖ Help you look at your emotions in a different way

❖ Bring relief and healing to you through your emotions

❖ Become aware of your emotions and how they are driving your life

❖ Accept this emotional journey as part of the human experience

❖ Know that you are not alone on this journey

❖ Understand that you can achieve emotional peace of mind

❖ Embrace a more effective way to approach life

❖ Achieve your goals AND enjoy the journey

❖ Understand that your beliefs are driving your emotions

❖ Help you see that when your life isn't working the way you'd like there are beliefs in the way that are creating your emotional state, and this keeps you stuck physically, emotionally, mentally, and spiritually

❖ Learn to own your emotional experience and don't expect anyone else to take responsibility for your emotional state. Wouldn't you like to be around more people that express this? So the place to start is yourself — you are the only one you can control.

THE PROCESS OF THIS BOOK

Please take your time and allow yourself to digest the material and integrate the changes in each chapter. Each chapter comes with its own affirmations you can align with and the tools to do it. Think of these affirmations in the way that best serves you. They could be intentions, goals, inspirational thoughts, or prayers.

The affirmations will quickly integrate into your subconscious mind. Follow the process. This means you are not using your willpower to keep the affirmations constantly in mind. Instead, they become the new thoughts that are constantly playing in the background of your day.

Use Selected Movies to See How Each Chapter Applies in Real Life

"I love the capacity that film has to teach. It's a very powerful medium. It forces you to take a look inside sometimes and when you leave the theater, occasionally you're changed."[1]—Renee Zellweger

The movies we suggest will allow you to experience a different culture, belief system, and way of living from the inside out. When you watch the movies we suggest, come from the context of how it's discussed in the book so you can get the understanding we're trying to convey. Even if you've seen the movie in past, look for the messages we present and try not to just approach it from a solely entertainment perspective.

Use the Selected Music Lists

The music lists reinforce the themes of each chapter, along with suggested essential oils and other tools. The direction above on how to watch the movies also applies to listening to the suggested music.

"There's definitely something healing in music, not only for the person singing, but also for the people listening. There's something that you're transmitting that isn't there when you sing.... It's all about vibration and the higher vibrations. It connects us to something beyond our understanding."[2] —Sting

Use Essential Oils as a Natural Way to Help with the Emotions

Essential oils have no side effects – they are all natural and powerfully healing.

"Both learning and healing are optimal when all parts of the mind, soul, and personality are engaged in a creative process. Inhaling a beautiful oil stimulates an opening of the mind–body connection..."[3] We use essential oils simply because they work for us.

Disclaimer: When sourcing the recommended uses of essential oils, these statements have not been evaluated by the U.S. Food and Drug Administration. These products are not intended to diagnose, treat, cure, or prevent any disease.

The movies, music, and oils are your tools to assist you on your emotional journey while reading this book. These suggested tools will help you to integrate the emotional awareness you may experience, so use them when it feels right. What can you expect after energizing your affirmations? Thinking differently creates different actions and produces new results. This book is about generating your inner wisdom. Wisdom is applied knowledge. We've created this book in a way that provides opportunities for wisdom. The suggested movies provide the knowledge in a way that also leverages your time.

INTRODUCTION

The dragons of which we speak are our emotions and what we create with our emotional responses. We want you to know that all these emotions are beneficial. The key is for your emotions to work for you, in harmony. What does that mean?

It means that you have to make friends with every single one of them. You have to allow every single one of your emotions the space to be expressed and felt.

It does not mean wallowing in them for hours on end. It is more about recognizing what you are feeling, acknowledging it, and knowing what to do with it. It also does not mean that you get to throw your emotions at other people; that is not their purpose. The emotions are here to teach us. As one Persian proverb says: "One pound of learning requires ten pounds of common sense to apply it." Our intention is to give you a commonsense way of taming your dragons.

Sue-Anne's Journey

I have always had a love of dragons. If you saw my home, you'd laugh – I have dragons everywhere. Dragons for me can be gentle and fierce. Other people have dogs for protection; I have dragons, and they are my protectors and friends. I love the way dragons come in all sizes, colors, and temperaments. They can be found curled up like a cat or flying with great power. I especially like the way dragons are found wrapped around the feet of Quan Yin.

In many traditions, Quan Yin is one of the most beloved deities. She is the embodiment of compassionate loving kindness. I have always felt a strong and personal connection to her (and you'll find many Quan Yins in my home too). I think of Quan Yin as the Buddhist equivalent of Mother Mary in Christianity. To me, she reminds me to stay in my heart, expressing compassion and love.

As a little girl, I was always told that I was too sensitive, that I wore my heart on my sleeve, and that I was just way too emotional. My life has been a journey to understand how to work with my emotions and feelings. The question kept coming up: Are my emotions different from my feelings? What I've come to understand is that emotions are what I experience on the surface and feelings are my deeper state of being.

Think of what it's like when you're in the ocean or any body of water. The surface can be stirred by whatever weather is occurring at the time. If there's a strong wind blowing, you can see the white caps on the surface. In our everyday life, our environment stirs us, and our emotions are the effect of that stirring, just like the white caps on the water's surface. There's a deeper place a couple feet below the surface where the water is calm regardless of the weather outside. When you make peace with your emotions, you can remain calm below the surface, no matter what is occurring in your environment and what emotions are being generated. So think of your emotions as passing weather systems – they are valid, they have purpose, and they are temporary.

David's Experience

Early in my career at Ford, I was assigned to one of its largest and most profitable Lincoln-Mercury dealers. This dealership was known to be innovative in all areas of business, including interpersonal development. On my first day, I was asked to read a book by Scott Peck called, *A World Waiting to Be Born: Civility Rediscovered*. The general manager explained that building a community in the workplace was a priority in his organization and if I was going to join their team, I needed to learn how to work in their community. He went on to explain that because of this book, their sales, customer satisfaction, and profits had reached all-time highs. The dealership believed that working together on teams using Scott Peck's ideas was transforming business.

I was intrigued and accepted his offer. I was deeply moved by the book, so much so that I read it four times. I studied how it worked at the dealership, its strengths and its weaknesses. I witnessed a genuine effort to build community. Competing departments got to know each other, people expressed their feelings at all levels in the organization, and problems were resolved by diverse teams. The only downside was the emotional tumult that seemed to flare up from time to time. People would open up, only to find themselves struggling with what to do with the feelings they were experiencing. I always thought that the most difficult part of the concept was how to handle the emotions that were stirred. This experience was the seed for my passionate desire to take a working model of community into the larger workplace.

Eleven years later, I met Sue-Anne and began working with her. I felt that her work could be a powerful tool to assist teams in working together and addressing the emotional component. This led to Sue-Anne asking me to assist her with the writing of this book. But how would we express her knowledge and modalities in a way that anyone could experience? It occurred to us that movies and music could be the accessible vehicle to help others gain a new perspective. I was thrilled, because I felt that these tools could assist any group of people that wanted to improve working together.

I have been told that I am a complex man, which includes my emotions. It has been a challenge to understand, reveal, and express the depth and breadth of my emotional side. Like many men, I was comfortable in the realm of anger. We are taught that as men our job is to be strong and not show weakness. We're all supposed to "man-up," as the saying goes. Any emotion other than anger is considered unmanly. I saw writing this book with Sue-Anne as a way to make working with the emotions accessible and acceptable for both men and women.

I no longer avoid or fear any emotion, including anger, and I have become more comfortable with who I am. It takes courage to be willing to open up this way as a man, but the upside is worth it. I believe it has allowed me to connect easier with others, to understand the feminine expression better, and improved my abilities as a leader.

The world is going through some of the greatest changes in modern history. Perhaps this work will help us all adjust to these changes more quickly and discover win-win outcomes along the way.

CHAPTER 1

All Emotions Serve

"Some stories don't have a clear beginning, middle, and end.
Life is about not knowing, having to change, taking the moment
and making the best of it, without knowing what's going to
happen next. Delicious ambiguity..." – Gilda Radner

The intent of this book is not to have a theoretical discussion on emotions. It is meant to give some insight into our emotional side and how we can make use of it. There is nothing inherently wrong with any emotions. All the emotions have purpose; there are no bad emotions. We can say that all your emotions are on an equal plane in a sense, because they are all indicators of where you are.

Feelings, Mental States, and Emotions

For our purposes in this book, we use the terms *feelings, mental states,* and *emotions* interchangeably. A *feeling* is how an emotion is registered in the body, a physical sensation. For example, something feels hot or cold.

Emotion is defined as a *mental state* that arises spontaneously rather than through conscious effort and is often accompanied by physiological changes. The word's origin is from the mid-sixteenth century French: *emouvior* based on the Latin *e* (out) + *movere* (move).

Emotion is energy in motion – "e" for energy + "motion." Every emotion sends out a specific, powerful vortex of energy. There is an old saying: "Energy follows thought." This means that when you have a thought there is an energy outburst that quickly follows it – this is the emotion. The type of energy is determined by the emotions associated with that thought (i.e., whether you like the thought or not).

For example, when you think, "I'm not good at this," can you feel the emotion? It is heavy and might be called resignation. When you think, "This is fun," can you feel the emotion? It is light and invites others to join in.

Think of being in a sports venue watching you favorite team. When the team is winning, there is great exuberance and everyone is jumping up and down. You feel elated. Now think of what happens when it goes south and your team starts to lose. Everyone gets quiet; it feels horrible and painful, and you leave the location feeling despondent.

Sue-Anne is an avid watcher of the Olympics. Back in 2000, when the Olympics were held in her hometown of Sydney, Australia, she was living in the United States. The swimming competitions were on, and it was Australia vs. the US in the 4 x 100 men's relay. Sue-Anne became so caught up in the emotion and energy of the crowd that she was on her feet in her living room, screaming at the top of her voice and cheering the Aussies on. She felt incredible as the Aussies touched the Americans out for the win. This boost of energy was a high that lasted for days – and of course her American husband, Dr. Tom Lenahan, had to listen to her crowing for days too. This is what is meant by energy in motion. The excitement is conveyed across time and space. In fact, the energy was going out around the world and available for anyone to tune into.

Equally powerful is what happens when you are watching a movie that terrifies you. For many of us in the US, that was the movie *Jaws*. Many who watched this movie even today have an irrational fear of sharks. In fact, all they need to hear are the first few base notes of the music, and there's a physical reaction. Sue-Anne, who grew up with shark nets around many Australian beaches, doesn't relate to this fear, and it doesn't generate the same reaction. In reality, a person has a much higher chance of being killed in a car accident than being eaten by a great white shark, yet these thoughts and behaviors persist because of the emotion that is stuck in the body.

Why Do We Need to Look at Our Emotions?

Each of us has maximum energy available for our lives. If we refuse to look at our emotions, we can get derailed by them. Each emotion has a pattern of thought and a feeling that generated it. When we don't look at what's going on, the emotion stays in place and the emotional energy pings around inside us like a pinball machine, hitting all the areas of our life. When we are tired of the pinball machine, we just wall the emotions off; we freeze them in place and avoid any activity or topic of conversation that could possibly evoke that emotion. At times, we all unconsciously do this, and it takes energy to keep that wall in place. Think of how strong a dam has to be to contain the water it's holding back. When you dam up your emotions, you are walling off a piece of yourself, and you are reducing the amount of energy available to use in your life.

Why Do We Avoid Looking at Some or All of Our Emotions?

Each culture has a set of emotions that are condoned, and these are often defined by whether you're male or female. These cultural patterns are passed down through the generations until they become the norm. In the American culture, if you express anything outside of these norms of emotion, you're criticized for either being too emotional or not showing enough emotion. It's as if there's a rule book that we all adhere to so we can be considered normal. If you're British, it's "the stiff upper lip" that is valued. Then there are the Italians, who openly express their emotions with each other and through their art and music. In many cultures, we think our emotions demean us. We now try to measure our intelligence by how we can control our emotions.

In the last fifteen years, science and business have been on a journey of discovery to pinpoint the usefulness of discerning the emotions and how they apply to the workplace. Companies throughout the world use aptitude tests to estimate a person's emotional aptitude or emotional intelligence, with the hope of using these as a predictor of workplace and leadership potential. Daniel Goleman, author of the international best seller *Emotional Intelligence*,[4] has inspired corporations to see the value of emotions as a different form of intelligence. When we are aware of emotional intelligence, we want to make sure we don't give off too many emotional clues that may impede our current success or prevent us from landing the right job. Perhaps we try to hide our emotions as much as possible so we can keep progressing. We may feel we have to keep our guard up so we're not overcome by what we consider to be the unpredictability of our emotions.

Many times, we avoid looking at our emotions because we fear that we'll upset others or be derailed if we express them. If we don't acknowledge them, then we can pretend they're not there and push them inwards until they appear to have gone away.

In the movie *Life or Something Like It*,[5] we see an example of a woman who is ignoring her emotions and doesn't want to acknowledge them. Lanie Kerrigan, played by Angelina Jolie, is a local Seattle TV news reporter who is told by a homeless man that she will die within a week. At first, she doesn't believe him, but after several of his other predictions come true, she is terrified that his prophecy about her is about to come to pass. Finally, she completely lets go, drops her guard, and does her morning report live while intoxicated from the prior night. She has so much fun with the people in her report that she gets attention from the national media and has an opportunity to be promoted to the New York bureau. At this point in the story, she starts to face into her discontent with her life, and she allows her emotions to be acknowledged. She accepts that she's not really happy with the relationship with her pro-baseball fiancé, and she starts questioning everything in her life in terms of how it makes her feel. We get to watch what happens when she follows these feelings and how they play out in her professional and personal life.

Lanie starts to make conscious choices for herself based on whether something increases her feelings of contentment and joy.

In the movie *Finding Forrester*,[6] we view an example of how this plays out with a man. William Forrester, played by Sean Connery, has gotten stuck in his emotions. They are essentially frozen. He doesn't leave his apartment, he drinks to cover his pain, and he doesn't allow himself the joy of seeing the birds he loves at the park. He refuses to talk about his past, his family, or his successful book. He's stuck in the regret he felt about his brother after WWII. He lives his life as a recluse. He ends up being emotionally stuck in his disappointments for over fifty years, only able to relive the sadness and regrets with a limited range of emotion and life experience. "He talked a little less and drank a little more," Forrester says about his brother. "The rest of those who have gone before us cannot steady the unrest of those to follow," Jamal (the young teen who befriends him) replies, quoting Forrester's work.

The Emotional Continuum

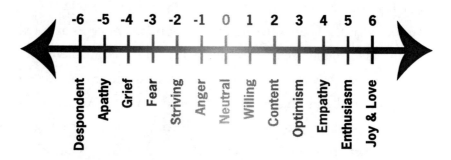

Emotions are typically divided into two categories: good and bad. We have this idea that emotions such as despondency, anger, grief, and fear are bad and should be avoided at all cost. This is truly not the case. They are seen as bad because they are often expressed in a destructive way. Each emotion is a point on a scale that starts with the most negative emotion and ends with the most positive emotion you can think of. We've created the following emotional continuum, or number line, to show how this works. The rank and order of these emotions aren't meant to be set in stone – they are simply used for discussion purposes. The rank and order will have variances based on each person's individual emotional system and life patterns.

Each emotion has a purpose. Each one lets us know where we are on the continuum and what thoughts we have been listening to. See this continuum as a number line – you can be at one, or you can be at minus one. What we usually consider to be negative emotions are just a reference point on the other end of the scale. When you understand that there is nothing wrong with being at negative five, that it's simply a reference point for where you are so you can gauge which direction you are going, then you don't judge how you feel.

However, you do not want to hang out in these negative numbered emotions for long periods of time. When you do, you will be creating more of the same feelings, because your focus intensifies them. So, when you have gone there, just remember that this is only a marker of where you are, like a street sign – nothing more, nothing less. If you continue to think about it – for example, "I am angry, and I don't wish to be here, and I should be somewhere different," then you only intensify your position. It's like staking a claim on that negative space, and you will continue to experience more of that space. Some of us get stuck in this space, while others will generate enough momentum to slide further down the negative aspect of the scale. In the example of being angry, for instance, a person might land somewhere around fear, grief, or despondency.

Ideally, you want to focus on something that will move you up the emotional scale. You're looking for something that eases the current emotion you are feeling. Your goal is to continue to take steps that increase this ease until you can at least get to a neutral space. You are seeking the place where you feel some balance and an ability to respond rather than react. We all have the ability to choose whichever space we find ourselves in. Whether you are in negative six, or three, or four, or five – it doesn't matter. Right where you are is the point of choice, and that is the space where you begin.

But if you cannot recognize where you are, then how can you move? We all need references points to know which way to go, just like we use maps to navigate. If you are walking on a trail through the bush or through woods, you need to know where you are to know where you are going. When you see a specific pond, it lets you know that you need to head to your right or to your left. This continuum simply provides an understanding of the relativity of emotions; it is your map. When you can recognize your emotional marker, then remember not to make things more difficult by judging where you are. Self-judgment adds intensity, marks the space, exhausts you, and can ultimately send you back down the scale.

We often think that we should be hanging out in bliss, joy, and excitement all the time. This is admirable, but unfortunately it's not very realistic for most of us. So, instead of embracing how we are feeling, we try to deny our feelings and paint over these unwanted emotions with pink paint. We then show the world and ourselves the sanitized version of our feelings – we pretend we are feeling good. This may work in the short term, but in the long term it prevents us from being able to genuinely hang out in joy and bliss.

Your Emotions Are Your Power Source

Emotions unite all parts of your system: body, mind, and soul. Think of them as a power source that goes very deep within the body. You have your spiritual part, your mental part, and your physical part. The emotions are the way that you connect all these parts. They have great power. If you do not acknowledge them, you negate the very part of yourself that wishes to be integrated. As *New York Times* columnist David Brooks says about selecting supreme-court justices:

"... Decisions are made by imperfect minds in ambiguous circumstances. It is incoherent to say that a judge should base an opinion on reason and not emotion because emotions are an inherent part of decision-making. Emotions are the processes we use to assign value to different possibilities. Emotions move us toward things and ideas that produce pleasure and away from things and ideas that produce pain... the emotions serve as guidance signals, like from a GPS, as you feel your way toward a solution."[7]

Acknowledge the fact that all emotions are trying to tell you something. Emotions let you know what your current interpretation means to you. They also let you know what your gut feeling is telling you. Ideally, you want to come to a point where you trust your emotional response, instead of ignoring it, which is what typically happens to most of us. We've been taught that some of the emotions are acceptable and some are bad, and this varies based on our home and culture. Socially acceptable people only allow that society's so-called good emotions to be expressed. There's also a clear distinction of which emotions are acceptable for men and which ones for women.

For many people, anger isn't allowed because it upsets those around us. This is especially true for women. As a result, we defer to someone else's feelings and bury the anger. If you allow the negative emotions to be expressed, people might become upset and may not like what your feeling means to them. Remember, there is nothing wrong with what you are feeling, and you are not responsible for another person's perception. Their perception of your feelings is only *their* perception. They are taking it personally rather than allowing you to feel what you feel.

Your goal is to allow yourself to feel what you feel and then discern what generated the feeling. What is your body, mind, and spirit actually saying? Is it allowing you to process something you don't understand? Is it allowing you to see that perhaps you have gone astray? Have you made an interpretation that produced anger but does not really serve you? Is it allowing you to see that you made an interpretation that will lead to peace? Is it allowing you to see the grooves in which you regularly get stuck? Think of your emotion as the spice of life – why not use the whole range?

Your Emotional Grooves

Grooves are similar to four-lane highways that have been created over time and used over and over again. Think of these highways as the grooves of thought, the grooves of action, and the grooves of perspective. Over time, we create these emotional grooves through how we've experienced life. Ideally, you want to create grooves that serve you better and smooth over the ones that cause detours. How long you spend in your emotional grooves and how intense they are will reveal the depth and strength of your grooves. When you recognize the grooves in your life and how you react to them, you're on your way to creating new highways or pathways that serve you better. Usually, you recognize these grooves in others before you can see them in your own life, and that's okay.

Every emotion can become a groove. Let's take a look at the groove of anger. If you're one that slips into this groove, your anger lets you know that perhaps you have headed off on a detour. You're most likely taking the long way to get where you want to go. Anger is a longer path, because we normally don't view anger as simply a marker. As a result, the anger groove can actually cloud your ability to make a good choice for yourself.

Remember, the emotions interact with your mind, body, and spirit, so the emotion of anger puts a fog around your whole energetic system. This makes it challenging to determine good choices, and this is why anger can sometimes be the longer route to your destination. You get stuck in the groove and can't get clear on how to get back on track again. When you come to understand that these emotions are just markers, you can respond by saying, "Oh, I have gone in a direction that is perhaps not serving me" – rather than wallowing in the emotion, allowing it to become even more intense in the process, going deeper and deeper in the groove.

Remember, there is nothing wrong with feeling anger or any other emotion. You want to feel it long enough to recognize where you are so you can discern the next right action for you. The longer you take in the groove creates a detour from your desired destination. Anger is there so you can recognize the need to make a better choice for yourself. Perhaps it is simply a different interpretation that is required.

Which Grooves Are Serving You, and Which Are Not?

There are grooves for the different areas of your life. There is a groove for your mate, for your business environment, how you respond to your siblings, etc. Think of all the ways you can break up your life into different areas and different domains – you will discover emotional grooves that have been created in each of these. These grooves of belief all lead to emotional output.

Emotional grooves are not necessarily bad. They are just grooves of thought, action, and perceptions. Our goal is to find out which of these grooves are serving you and which are not, because grooves can become unconscious. It is similar to your favorite route to work. Does it ever feel like the car is driving itself? That is because the groove is so deep in your system that your whole body operates without even having to consciously be aware of it. Grooves only cause us problems when they become grooves of reaction on a day-to-day basis. Your grooves then create a consistent way of having an emotional reaction to something. The emotion is consistent because you have the same sequence of thoughts. When something happens and it appears to be like an event from your past, the same sequence of thoughts kick in, you jump into that groove, and away it goes. It's not unlike going down a waterslide (or a slippery dip if you're an Aussie!). You're at the top, you see something that rattles you, and then – whoosh – you are down that waterslide.

Ideally, you want to catch yourself before you react and slide into your groove. When you are aware of where you are in the moment and what you are feeling, you are on your way to more choices in your life. You are no longer unconscious and merely reacting. When we live reactively, our grooves become like Pavlov's dogs. When they rang the bell in Pavlov's experiment, the dogs would salivate. This is not unlike what we do in our grooves. The good news is that there are ways to catch yourself before you slide.

First, you have to be conscious of what you are feeling; hence the marker. The marker allows you to recognize where you are on the continuum. Notice that, once in the groove, you find more things to deepen it through justifications found on the Internet, social networking, blogs, smart phones, complaining to others, or the nonstop news that's ubiquitous these days. This is what happens when you do not interrupt these grooves. You effectively deepen the groove by seeking external justification, and you do this because you think it will soothe you. Repetition deepens the groove and increases the difficulty of finding a way out. Think about your habits – some are easier to change than others. Typically, the longer the habit, the harder it is to change. So, the energy relates to the depth of the groove; it's all about your level of awareness. As Eckhart Tolle writes in his book, *The Power of Now:* "As you become more conscious of your present reality, you may suddenly get certain insights as to why your conditioning functions in those particular ways."[8]

Next, make friends with this awareness of where you are. If you sit and judge yourself for having driven into an unconscious groove, you actually deepen the groove. You are matching the emotion of where you are, and now you are deepening it, which doesn't serve you. It's similar to the story about the donkey and the well that circulated the Internet several years ago:

One day a farmer's donkey fell down into a well.

The donkey cried piteously for hours as the farmer tried to figure out what to do. Finally, he decided the animal was old, and the well needed to be covered up anyway; it just wasn't worth it to retrieve the donkey.

He invited his neighbors to come over and help him. They each grabbed a shovel and began to shovel dirt into the well. At first, the donkey realized what was happening and cried horribly. Then, to everyone's amazement, he quieted down.

A few shovel loads later, the farmer finally looked down the well. He was astonished at what he saw. With each shovel of dirt that hit his back, the donkey was doing something amazing. He would shake it off and take a step up.

As the farmer and his neighbors continued to shovel dirt on top of the animal, he would shake it off and take a step up. Pretty soon, everyone was amazed as the donkey stepped up over the edge of the well and happily trotted off!

In this story, the donkey initially fights against what is happening. When he calms down and accepts what is going on, he discovers a way out of his predicament. All he has to do is continue to shake off the dirt (the feelings), and keep taking the next step, which gets him the outcome he desires. This applies to all of us when we recognize we've slipped into one of our grooves.

When David was editing this section, he experienced an example of how quickly we can fall into a groove. David was working on the book, and he knew he was tired, so he decided to take a break and check his personal accounts online. Normally, this is not an issue, but this time he saw there was only $25 in his checking account. This was a surprise to him, because he's always on top of his financial details. He quickly slipped into a place of depression, wondering how this could have happened. He began feeling down about where he and his family were financially vs. their goals. Many of us have experienced this groove of financial despair. It doesn't matter if we're talking about having only $25 in our account, or $15,000. It's a matter of perspective.

Money and sex are two of the biggest collective grooves on our planet today. Even those with great fortunes fall into these grooves. For example, Will Smith told Oprah: "… No matter how successful you get, it's really difficult to shake your mindset, and I still have a poor person mentality I can't shake, and it gets really detrimental when you can't just shake off the ideas. When I go to sleep right now, I am as financially nervous as I was twenty years ago."[9] Will Smith's mindset is a groove, and it reminds us that money can be a big groove for all of us.

Working with these grooves in a balanced way requires focus and perseverance. Since David was in the middle of editing this chapter, he was able to recognize that he had slid into a financial groove again. At this point, he did things to distract himself and move up the emotional continuum. He left his home and picked up some groceries for dinner. Lura, his spouse, made a beautiful meal, and he enjoyed this with his family and some friends. Then they watched one of their favorite TV programs. The result was that he felt better, and he was pleased that he had caught himself so quickly and had recognized that this financial groove still had some depth.

Sometimes we think there's a quick fix for these grooves; we think that just like taking a couple of aspirin, we will instantly feel better again. Usually this isn't the case; you have to slowly fill in your groove over time, seeing what works for you along the way. Remember, it's taken much time and energy to create some of these grooves – especially financial ones. As a result, it takes time to fill them in and learn new ways to address them. Be patient with yourself and allow yourself time to heal these places.

We Tell Our Story Over and Over and Become Identified with It

It is better to say, "I am healing, and emotion is just working itself out of my body." You want to allow the emotion to release and the healing to begin without creating more of it by reliving your story.

Dr. Ernest Holmes wrote a book called *The Voice Celestial*. He gives the example of a man with a headache. As long as he focuses on the headache, he'll never get to the cause.

When we perceive something as bad – an event, a person, a memory, etc. – and we feel like we have no control over it, it then produces the emotions that send us down the continuum of anger, fear, and grief. This is the point where we have a choice in this emotion.

How Do We Learn from Our Emotions?

We learn by staying there long enough to recognize where we are. When you do this, you make better choices by recognizing your body's reactions, not just your thoughts. You become aware of what your different senses are telling you: how things feel, look, and sound, and what that means. This becomes a lifelong practice as you get to know yourself better and better. When you can understand what your emotions are telling you, you're able to make friends with them. You create rapport, just like you do with people. Remember, it takes more energy to contain your emotions than to flow with them in the moment.

The Emotions Are an Overture to Peace of Mind

We all desire happiness. What we don't realize is that peace of mind is the pathway to sustained happiness. We want happiness in our finances, our relationships, our careers, our homes, our marriages, our families, and our spiritual lives. Sometimes we fall into the "if only" trap of thinking; it goes something like this: "If only I can get the right job, or promotion, or spouse, or house, or wealth, then I'll be at peace and I will be happy." Intuitively we know that money (or any other exterior thing) doesn't bring happiness. But it's much easier to pursue something external than to look within for peace and happiness.

When David worked for Ford, he had several opportunities to hang out socially with high-level executives. The nature of the work sometimes required dealer social trips (off-site meetings, fishing, golfing, skiing, etc.). During these times, some of the executives would begin to relax, and David got to learn about their lives. He'd hear how difficult it was to have to move their families from one part of the country to another. Or how much their lives were completely consumed by the job with its long hours and extensive travel. They were in constant upheaval and never knew if or when it would end. While a couple of executives loved what they did, David was surprised how many seemed unfulfilled. Most people think that the pathway to happiness and security is attaining one of these powerful positions. Yes, it brought prestige and financial benefits, but life balance was not encouraged. Dedication to business alone was worn as a badge of honor, displaying how committed they were to the company.

In this book, we invite you to discover practices you can use to look within that will enhance whatever external journey you are on. When you understand your emotions, make friends with them, and see how they're guiding you, then you can sustain peace of mind for longer periods. By taking this journey, you can discover how to be at peace wherever you are. Regardless of who you are married to or what company you work for, it's your emotional centeredness that leads to peace. When you can understand yourself from an emotional standpoint, you'll discover how your emotions can introduce you to peace regardless of what is going on in your life. Peace is an inside job, and our external lives can't provide the shortcut to the happiness that we all desire.

When we set out to achieve anything in our external lives, we can lose our peace of mind if we become attached to achieving our goal. We know we're attached when the goal matters more than anything else. We are actually taught that this is the way to be successful. Our whole life's focus is on the pursuit of the goal, and we want it as soon as possible. This attachment limits our perception of the way our goal can be obtained. It leads to looking for shortcuts, or doing whatever it takes to attain the goal. We get consumed by this attachment and lose our peace of mind. We see this when people commit crimes, resulting in incarceration and the loss of freedom – they didn't see any other way to achieve their goal. Others pursue financial success or security with such an intense focus that everything else in their life remains on hold until this elusive goal is attained. In this way, they also lose their freedom. The pursuit of a goal is a good thing; it is the attachment to the goal that limits our options. When we can find peace wherever we are, it opens us up to more opportunities at sustained happiness.

To achieve this type of peace and happiness consistently takes practice. Anyone that achieves mastery in anything – be it playing an instrument or becoming a professional athlete, actor/director, corporate executive, or teacher – takes practice. Mastery in any external activity doesn't come overnight, and neither does the internal mastery of peace. If you have been able to achieve mastery in any external life activity, then you already have the context of what we're saying. When you can apply your understanding of practice to internal mastery, you'll recognize that there are no shortcuts. It takes consistency, motivation, and courage, but it's worth it. Not only will you feel more peace and happiness in your life, but your external achievements will be more fulfilling too.

Classically trained musicians typically spend six to eight hours a day practicing their instrument during college and graduate studies. While this commitment takes much dedication and time, once they attain a certain set point, it becomes easy to return to it when preparing for each concert. They no longer require intense study because they've reached a level of expertise – their set point.

As John Favreau says, "I've been very fortunate that lightning has struck a number of times for me, but the lesson has changed. My life has gone from running to get to a destination to really trying to enjoy the journey."[10] When your internal practice gets better, you'll feel a growing sense of freedom – and once you get a taste of it, you'll never want to go back. This internal freedom will then help you to be an even better athlete, director, teacher, parent, executive, musician, etc., and you'll be able to sustain your expertise longer. We invite you to join us on this journey. ◈

❈ CHAPTER SUMMARY ❈

"When I was young, I found out that the big toe always ends up making a hole in a sock. So I stopped wearing socks" —Einstein

Wisdom is expansive because it provides access to new ways and choices of how you want to live your life. When you begin to discover the power of your emotions, you are on your way to finding the harmony that can open you up to peace in all the areas of your life.

BELIEF STATEMENTS REPRESENTED IN THIS CHAPTER:

Energizing Beliefs

- ❖ When I let my guard down, emotion flows and no longer builds up, looking for an outlet.

- ❖ If I let my guard down and allow God into all areas of my life, then everything will be all right and will work out better than I could have imagined.

- ❖ I seek to understand and don't rely on my assumptions.

- ❖ I never imagined I'd actually get to realize my dreams.

- ❖ When I experience friction with others, I look for the valuable lessons being presented and learn from them.

- ❖ I cherish the life lessons that I've received in my life.

- ❖ I write the first draft with my heart and rewrite with my head.

- ❖ I allow others to encourage me to get out of my comfort zone and experience new things.

- ❖ I don't write or speak for the critics, or just to be accepted.

- ❖ The only one who has to think I'm special is me; I just have to be myself — who I really am.

- ❖ I listen for the background story and don't get distracted by the words.

- ❖ I overcome my racial prejudices.

De-energizing Beliefs

❖ I don't think I've ever been wrong.

❖ There are some areas of my life where I just can't let go and allow God's grace to influence me.

❖ I don't want to have to talk about my emotions and would rather keep all conversations about logical issues.

❖ I misinterpret my guidance.

❖ I do just enough to not stand out; I do just enough to get by.

❖ Nobody should ever mess with me or my stuff.

❖ I'm bummed because things don't seem to be working out for me.

❖ I let people rattle me and affect my game.

❖ I have to live up to other people's standards and expectations.

❖ People judge me because of my race.

❖ When someone challenges me, I have to win.

MUSIC SELECTIONS

Tchaikovsky, "Symphony No. 5 in E Minor, Op. 64," Andante Maestros "It Won't Be Like This for Long," Darius Rucker

"Humble Me," Norah Jones

"Love So Right," The Bee Gees

"Rise," sung by Eddie Vedder

ESSENTIAL OIL RECOMMENDATIONS[11]

Orange: A 1995 Mie University study found that citrus fragrances boosted immunity, induced relaxation, and reduced depression.

Peppermint: Purifying and stimulating to the conscious mind.

Vetiver: Psychologically grounding, calming, and stabilizing. It helps us cope with stress and recover from emotional trauma.

Legacy: Contains a sampling of all single oils, reflecting the inclusion of all emotions.

Transformation: This empowers and upholds the changes you want to make in your belief system.

CHAPTER 2

Your Emotional Thermostat

How Do I Know What I'm Feeling in Each Area of My Life?

In each of these areas, you have what we've referred to as a set point – a place where you usually reside. What we mean by this set point is that it's a point at which you naturally gravitate to. It does not mean that it is where you will be all the time, but it is your natural gravitation. In a sense, if you think of it in terms of the grooves, you can say a certain depth of the groove is where you typically hang out. Sometimes you will go deeper, sometimes you will go lighter, but that is your natural place. When you recognize these inner set points, next you want to find a way that you can lighten them up, so you don't have to go so deep.

You might want to think of this in terms of a groove in the road that you fall into. Remember when a groove gets too deep? Workers come in and fill up the pothole. Think in the same way of your emotional self. You'll want to discover ways that you come in and fill up these grooves in your road. In other words, you are filling up the pothole you created so that you can create a different set point within yourself. It is a point of reference, once again.

You can also think in terms of a thermometer. Here, your set point is the point where you naturally adjust the thermostat in your home. It's summertime and extremely hot outside, so you set your thermostat at 80 degrees. When it gets down to 79 degrees, the thermostat turns off; once it comes back to 80, it's fine – and if it gets to 81, it turns on again. It's the same inside of you. You float around a particular set point in any area of your life. You have an overall set point for your emotional state, and another set point for your whole body. You also have individual set points that make up the different spheres of your life. Ideally, you want to work on them all simultaneously. It is important to work on your overall set point, but it is also important to address the individual areas.

Emotional Grooves in the Different Facets of Life

Your set point is the point of your natural gravitation and the depths of your grooves. Each individual has his/her own melting point, similar to glass. Each individual looks through their own kaleidoscope and takes a turn or a twist that changes how they see things, and this affects the whole. When our perspective changes, we change, and the community around us changes.

For now, think in terms of a specific area you would like to address, such as your relationship with your mate. You find that some of the ways your mate reacts can get you to go very deep into your groove, very quickly. What is that car analogy? 0 to 60 in 5.6 seconds? Think in terms of that analogy. What you want to do is to change it so it is no longer your set point. That way, as soon as you start talking to your mate on a contentious issue, you are automatically off and running. You want to find a way to diffuse the issue somewhat. For instance, you can take deep breaths so that you relax your body in the moment. You know it's a contentious issue, so you immediately call a time out and start doing some breathing for yourself.

There are a number of other modalities (tools) that we could suggest that you could be doing right then to calm your system down. What you are ultimately doing is not unlike the thermostat in your home. You want to change the setting. In other words, you may want to cool it down, and you want a new set point. Instead of a warm 80, you want to move it down to 78 so that this becomes your norm. Perhaps you will learn to cool it down even more so 76 degrees becomes the place you hover around. This becomes your set point in this specific area until you can get it to the place where you can stay neutral as you flow through. You can have discussions that would normally have been contentious in the past, but now you are able to smile and discuss the issue without getting overheated.

How We Freeze Our Emotions

We've all heard the analogy that men go into their cave and find a way to anesthetize themselves. There are many ways men do this. One is watching sports – any kind of sports. This can be a healthy or an unhealthy way of dealing with their emotions. Remember, all of these things are a continuum, and none are an end unto themselves. If you watch sports as a way to allow yourself to release some of your emotions, some of the places within that are frozen, then that is good and it serves you. However, if you spend up to ten of your waking hours doing nothing but watch sports, that might not be a good solution. You may now be using it to anesthetize yourself. One is a choice; the other is an unconscious reaction.

In general, men use alcohol, cigarettes, and sex. Anything that you think of as an addiction is a reaction. Men have a stronger propensity to addictions, in the sense that they become addicted to one of these ways and think they are responding, when they are actually reacting. Other examples are video games and watching movies. You could say this stems from a masculine way of trying to fix things. These addictions become their "system" for fixing themselves. Their addiction becomes their system for dealing with what ails them, and they think it is fixing things, but the opposite is true.

The way women freeze is to go into community and hang out with other women. Notice, though, if they find a supportive group, those women will call them on their crap and will not let them stay in a place of wallowing and constant discussion of what is wrong. So many women talk about what is wrong with their men. It gets deeper and deeper and deeper. What are they really doing? They are supporting each other in creating a deeper rut or groove. This is an example of reactivity instead of quiet responding.

Some women complain to other women in a way that reinforces their anger response. While they may feel this connects them with other women, it actually aids in freezing their emotions, and this deepens the groove. They end up reinforcing the belief that generates the anger emotion, and now this emotion is justified and the reactivity continues. They don't realize that these feelings have been generated by the recent beliefs they were thinking. They make it a closed loop, and they keep it going around and around, like a dog chasing its tail.

Women also freeze their emotions in much more distracting ways. They focus on shopping, working out in a gym, or on how they look. They freeze their emotions through gossip, rumors, and assumptions. Women think that turning to their friends will give them some of the truth and support they need. They know that their friends will take their side and legitimize how they feel. However, sometimes this just whips up more reactivity, making it harder to gain clarity. As a result, they get stuck in the drama and are unable to move through the emotions at hand. If this becomes a habit, it can turn into a groove of dependency and reactivity. Friends are supportive when they hold you and each other in their greatness, with love, forgiveness, and grace. This way allows the emotion to release so it doesn't keep going.

Many times women turn to food to soothe their emotions. Obviously, this isn't exclusive to women. The key is to realize that any obsessive activity leads to addiction and a loss of choice. Take gossip, for instance. Gossip is like a closed system, or a pinball machine. The emotion gets thrown around back and forth and keeps going down the grooves, reinforcing them each time it has nowhere to go, and thus the energy builds. Eventually, the person gets exhausted and decides to shut the emotion down instead of releasing it. As a result, the emotion gets frozen in the body.

Meg Ryan plays Mary Haines in the movie *The Women*[12]. Mary has learned that her husband is having an affair. Her friends learn about the high profile affair through gossip at the nail salon at Sax Fifth Avenue. Mary's friends get emotionally involved in Mary's discovery, and we see numerous examples of how this activity plays into the freezing of their emotions. When Mary and her best friend, Sylvia (Annette Bening) start to call each other on their self-told lies, they begin to start helping each other. Each one gives the other permission to be real, to feel what they feel, and then help each other through it. Mary and Sylvia begin to let go of their emotions and release their pent-up energy. As Sylvia says, "This is exhausting." Of course it's exhausting, because the thawing has begun and the body starts to relax again. Clarity follows the release of the emotions.

When Edie (Debra Messing) has her baby, we see another example of how the friends' drama makes it harder for the birth mom. They mean well, but their reactivity makes the birth more chaotic and frenetic than it needs to be. As women, we do this to each other, and we're not even aware of it.

It can be tricky trying to discover our own ways of freezing the emotions. It leads to the question, "Now that I see, what do I do next?" You first want to avoid beating yourself up for where you have been and be peaceful and grateful for the new understanding that it is time for change. Keep yourself from immediately going to a place of judgment – there's no point in going there. Now is the time to look at the reasons why you've been feeling what you're feeling, and seek to discover what's really going on so you can move to a place of response instead of reactivity. When you can make these discoveries about yourself without judgment, you have more ability to catch yourself when you are tempted to judge others for not conforming to your past ways that got you here. Judgment does not work for yourself or others. When you discover this truth, it's an opportunity for more peace in your life.

Propping Up Illusions

An illusion is defined as an erroneous mental representation that seems like truth. Many times we create illusions in an attempt to avoid the emotions we're experiencing. We become trapped in these illusions, and we are not aware of them or how we created them.

We turn to religion and sacred writings (the Bible, the Torah, etc.) for a justification of how we are feeling and as a way to justify our behavior and our perception of what others' behavior should be. This just perpetuates our reactivity internally and externally with others. It starts to get complicated – justification, judgments, religions, good intentions, or drinking the Kool-Aid are all examples of how we prop up the illusions. The more we prop up our illusions, the more we defer the emotional pain until eventually our choice is taken away from us in the extreme.

Another way we prop up our illusions is by thinking that our emotional thermostat (set point) can be adjusted as quickly as the thermostat in our homes. We delude ourselves into thinking that everything will now be different because we desire a change or a new set point. We are unaware that our thermostat is locked and not able to be adjusted for the new temperature. Think about the thermostats you've seen in schools, offices, and public places. Notice how they are usually protected with a locked case. Many times it's secured in plastic case requiring a key. Sometimes it's guarded with a metal cage. Both prevent anyone from changing the temperature except for the person with the key. Think of this case as the way we prevent a change to our set point. Before we can begin to change, we have to remove some of the blocks so we have access to our own emotional system.

How Do You Open Up to a New Set Point?

Acceptance

First, you have to accept where you are and not rail against it. In the first chapter, we discussed the empowering effects of knowing where your marker is on the emotional scale. Being aware is a powerful first step, but once we've become aware, many of us don't like what we discover and want to resist it. As Byron Katie discovered, "I am a lover of what is, not because I'm a spiritual person, but because it hurts when I argue with reality. We can know that reality is good just as it is, because when we argue with it, we experience tension and frustration. We don't feel natural or balanced. When we stop opposing reality, action becomes simple, fluid, kind, and fearless."[13]

Compassion

When you begin accepting yourself and where you are, this leads you to the next step: compassion. It's our self-judgment and harshness that blocks our ability to melt our protective case, preventing the new set point we desire. These realizations can be painful, and many of us are so afraid of the pain that we avoid the opportunity to heal. This is the time to have comforting kindness for yourself and your process of learning. This is a time for tender mercy. "There are times in the spiritual life when it feels as if all the barriers we have erected to shield ourselves from the pains of the world crumbled," Jack Kornfield says in his book *After the Ecstasy, the Laundry.*[14] Kornfield speaks of the need for compassion toward oneself. "The need for such compassion is there in every journey, Buddhist or Hindu, Jewish or Christian... human suffering is central to the journey of grace and redemption." Gentle compassion for yourself will help you to keep the protective covering removed. This understanding will allow you to gain new insights as you progress through this book.

New Thinking

When you begin accepting where you are with compassion, it allows your feelings and emotions to influence the way you think. Now you can begin to look at the thoughts around the issues in your life that cause you the most pain and suffering. As Byron Katie says in *Loving What Is,*[15] "I've never seen a work or money problem that didn't turn out to be a thinking problem." In the following chapters, we'll cover some of the major issues that cause us pain, the thinking around these issues, and how this thinking affects our lives. By keeping your thermostat guard down, you'll be open to realizing a new emotional set point and increasing opportunities for peace of mind. When you can see that your old thinking is in the way, it can lead to awareness – which is an important step towards wisdom.

"True, you're a butterfly now, but you still think like a caterpillar."

This Is **Your** Journey

Remember, the reason why so many offices and schools protect the thermostats with coverings is to keep others from changing the temperature set point. When we set out on our journey of healing and discovery, we can so quickly slip into thinking, "My spouse needs this awareness," or "If only my mother would get this lesson, then I'd be happy." As you read the following chapters, if you find yourself thinking about how other people need these lessons, it's usually an indication that you need it too. As our grade school teachers would say, "Keep your eyes on your own paper." This will allow you to stay focused on your journey and will keep you from getting distracted. If you recognize undesirable traits in others, see it as a blessing that you now recognize in you.

In *The Legend of 1900,*[16] we see an example of clinging to illusions rather than accepting the change life offers us. Danny Boodmann T.D. Lemon 1900 (Tim Roth) has lived all his life on a luxury cruise liner. He was orphaned as a newborn and adopted by the crew. His skills as a jazz pianist entertain the crowds as the ship goes back and forth across the Atlantic between the US and Europe. 1900 is a dreamer and always imagined that someday he would leave his home on the water and find a new life on land. 1900 gets many opportunities to step off the ship and start a new life, but he hesitates and doesn't take action. As time goes on, the travel industry changes, and his ship is no longer needed.

This movie gives us insight into how difficult it can be for men to let go, especially in modern society. We just don't have the practice like we used to in times past. When we were an agrarian society, men had the experience of letting go because the farm was always changing. You had to say good-bye to the beloved pig so the family could eat or accept the loss of your milk cow because of some disease. Many times, the rain didn't come and all the crops were lost. But all these losses aside, men also had to deal with the cyclical patterns of the seasons. This is why when men lose their jobs today, their whole world comes crashing down. Their identities are often totally caught up in what they do and its predictable delivery of needed income on a consistent basis. When it's gone, the man loses all sense of who he is, along with his worth. *The Legend of 1900* shows us how difficult it can be to walk away from our comfortable life and embark on a new phase or adventure in our life.

In these contemporary times, women seem to have more experience in letting go, and they get to practice it with their monthly cycles and with child-rearing. No matter how attached they get to their children, they eventually grow up and live their own lives. However, because women have increasingly assumed masculine roles and positions, this regular practice of letting go is also diminishing. So many women want their bodies to have predictable results, from managing their periods to controlling their emotional balance. We want to have predictable results so we can succeed in a male-dominated world. This is a world that doesn't understand going with the natural flow of life. Managing the body and emotions through medications serve in the short-term, but in the long-term they take a toll and break the natural cycles of a woman's life, and possibly make letting go difficult in similar ways to men.

Emotional Overload

Often, the first stage of emotional overload is that we go numb. It's as if the energetic circuit breaker becomes so overloaded that it shuts down – similar to your home's electrical circuitry. We just can't handle any more, and so our emotional system shuts down. This is another way we freeze emotions in our body. We stop breathing to try to avoid the pain. When you stop breathing, you stay shallow; you're not breathing through the emotion, allowing it to move, and this can lead to numbness. We see 1900 experience moments like this in the movie. He wants to follow his love and to discover a new life in New York City, but he can't and becomes immobilized right at the moment of change. It's too much for 1900, and he shuts down without embracing the change that is before him.

All Choices in Life Have Energetic Consequences

Repressing any emotion causes harm to our energetic system. We desire control so much that we won't make the needed changes until it's our idea, and then we will give something new a try. The walls that keep others out also keep us in. We like our grooves because they feel comfortable, and it takes considerable inertia to make a change. It doesn't have to be this way. 1900 made his choice to stay on the ship, and the stark consequences of that choice play out. Haven't we all done this in one form or another in our lives? We know the job doesn't fit any longer, yet we stay put because we're afraid of change. Or sometimes it's our relationships – a spouse, a parent, or a child that we aren't willing to look at in order to seek a new dynamic. We lose our choice, and the consequences (being fired, divorced, etc.) seem to catch us off guard. The signs were usually there; we just refused to look at them. We bury our feelings about the issue, hoping it will somehow magically go away on its own.

A Life of Quiet Desperation

Many of us live in quiet despair. At times, we do not feel valued and worthy to be alive, perpetuating the self-loathing and despair. All we want is to be recognized by others. Some of us create pictures of how our lives should look. At the time, it seems like the right fit, and we go on with life, assuming this is the script we have to play out. We make commitments and rigidly insist there is no room to change them. Our identities get so tied up into being committed that we won't admit that, at the time we made choices, we didn't know what we didn't know. That's how we gain wisdom. It's trial and error. But if we're unwilling to change or even look at things, when quiet desperation sets in, we can get stuck. This happens when parts of ourselves can't have a voice because we simply don't allow it.

In the movie *Vicki Cristina Barcelona*,[17] Vicki has her life all planned out: she is ready to marry her dream husband and live the life of a wealthy woman. The summer before her wedding, she studies in Barcelona, Spain, with her opened-minded friend, Cristina. Vicki discovers a passion she wasn't aware of, and it causes her to question everything she thought was perfect for her life. She's afraid to follow her heart and simply doesn't have the courage to see where it will go. Many of us never get the opportunity to discover our passions, and we believe that we have to play the part in this life as is. We get so caught up in our cultural norms that we can't see what we're missing. Vicki gets a glimpse, by allowing herself to be immersed in another culture that's less rigid with more creative options. It's only then that she can allow herself to wonder if her life back home still fits.

As the narrator says, "Vicki went home to have her grand wedding to Doug, to the house they both finally settled on, and to lead the life she had envisioned for herself before the summer in Barcelona." This movie helps us to see how we make choices that forever direct the course of our lives. It shows how we seem to think that once we've made a choice, it's forever. This belief can lead us to limited variety and quiet desperation. When we discover new inner perspectives about ourselves, there are always ways to incorporate them into our lives. It takes courage to explore these new revelations, and it doesn't always have to result in chaos.

Working with Emotional Grooves

When we turn to our old ways of coping (alcohol, sex, sports, shopping, etc.), we reinforce our grooves and freeze the emotion. Sometimes it can be difficult to recognize how deep these grooves have become. Life has a way of sending you signs and indications that a groove needs to be filled in. Some of us get the message and reach out to others and support groups for help. However, many of us just aren't aware and continue along our way, believing that this is the best life has to offer us. It isn't until we experience enough pain that we recognize the groove. We call these experiences "two-by-four events," because it feels like a two-by-four just smacked you, and it hurts! In the movie *Crazy Heart*,[18] Bad Blake, portrayed by Jeff Bridges, is a country music singer that gets stuck playing dive bars. He is broke and addicted to alcohol and cigarettes. He's stuck in a groove, numb, and he doesn't know how deeply stuck he is until Jean Craddock, (Maggie Gyllenhaal) comes into his life. She's a ray of light and love that allows him to see how unhappy he is. While going to visit her (and probably drunk), he falls asleep and runs off the road. He ends up in the hospital, and Jean takes care of him. This is a two-by-four event that gives him an opportunity to change. Because of her, he starts to think about his life, and he reconciles with his son and his former music partner, Tommy Sweet (Colin Farrell) – although this isn't enough to get him completely out of the groove. It takes an incident involving Jean's son, who gets lost while Bad Blake was taking care of him. He stops to have a drink and before he knows it, the boy is gone. Jean leaves him, and his chance at love is lost. However, *this* is finally the two-by-four event needed to get him to seek help and go into rehab. He gets better, starts writing again, and begins touring with Tommy Sweet again. His life is better than ever, and he's happy.

Find ways to lighten up and smooth your own grooves so you don't have to go too deep. Remember, intensity can stop you dead in your tracks. The speed at which you hit the groove determines the speed you slow down. Have courage – you are strong enough to make the changes you desire. When you fall into a deep groove, it usually happens quickly. You don't know how you got there, and you can't see the light or a way out of the groove. So – what do you do? First, be grateful that you're aware of the situation, and then try to slow down. Create a segue – watch a movie, go for a walk, etc. Doing this will lighten your mood and give you an opportunity to discover what tripped you up so you can work on smoothing this particular groove so it doesn't have the same depth anymore.

Do I Have to Reset All Areas Before I Get Results?

When beginning the work on the grooves in your life, it's best to focus on just one area. Remember, this is a journey, not something to be accomplished all at once. One groove at a time is the best way to work with yourself – otherwise, it's like trying to learn how to juggle with too many balls in the air. You struggle to get the skill down, it gets too complicated, and then you give up. Think of it like balancing plates on a stick. If you have too many going at the same time, they all fall and break. It's just too difficult to change everything all at once, so don't put this burden on yourself – focus on only one area.

The Power of Distraction

When you begin working on a specific groove, you are on your way to relief and healing. Many of us get stuck with "what is" and can't seem to get off of it. Our attention remains on our groove and we won't let up. We ruminate about where we are or where we should be by now and end up digging deeper. Now is not the time to wallow in your current awareness – you'll just hold yourself back. This is why you need to create a distraction for yourself.

Distraction – we do it with children. Why? Because it works. Why not do the same when you've recognized that you're in a groove? Distraction can become the groove interrupt, the pause in the emotion that serves you. When you've started working on one area in your life that you want to improve, the other grooves can surface too and throw you off track. That's why we suggest finding ways to distract yourself, so you don't lose focus and give up. It will give you relief, so find ways that work for you that allow you to create the pause that distracts. Here are some suggestions that have worked for us:

❖ Go for a walk. It will calm the system and allow nature to take your mind off your reactivity.

❖ Stop what you're doing and breathe long breaths in and out without interruption.

❖ Get some rest – relax and let yourself be carried for a bit. Many times sleep is just what you need.

❖ Watch a movie.

❖ Call a supportive friend.

❖ Play with your pets.

- Meditate or pray.
- Utilize our essential oil suggestions.
- Listen to music from our provided list (or any music you love).
- Have a cup of tea or your favorite beverage and sit for a while.

These are just a few examples of how we distract ourselves. Have fun finding ways that fit you best.

CHAPTER SUMMARY

Are you wondering, where do I start? Begin by picking any area where you're noticing a pattern that you desire to change. Notice the intensity of the emotion and recognize this pattern is highlighting a set point. Use this chapter to help you begin the process of adjusting your thermostat. As you read the following chapters, be on the lookout for suggestions on how to work with your emotional grooves in ways that feel right to you. Filling in the grooves is an important step to realizing a new set point. You can't get it wrong, so go easy on yourself and take your time.

BELIEF STATEMENTS REPRESENTED IN THIS CHAPTER:

Energizing Beliefs

❖ Time passes so quickly that I choose to enjoy every moment now.

❖ I embrace a better life.

❖ I take life one day at a time.

❖ I'm good at writing and creating, and I love getting back to my art.

❖ I don't have to choose the hard way anymore.

❖ I find ways to put the spark back into my sexual relationship with my mate.

❖ I let my pain be comforted.

❖ I'm humble about my gifts.

❖ I let people help me to succeed.

❖ I allow myself to let go and move through my emotions.

❖ Who I'll be tomorrow is anybody's guess.

❖ There's nothing we can't talk about or try to resolve.

❖ I have the freedom to choose whatever I want from the buffet of life.

De-Energizing Beliefs

❖ I like being the bad guy.

❖ It's easier to get my status from my father and husband than doing something myself.

❖ I wish I had a rule book to give me the answers I seek.

❖ It's hard to be my friend.

❖ Life sucks and then you die.

❖ If I make this change, I'll feel like I have to play life with two right arms.

❖ My marriage isn't enough for me.

❖ This whole thing about finding peace and happiness will pass.

❖ I have to choose security.

❖ My mate will never reach his/her full potential.

❖ I don't want to live; my head is going to explode; I can't live like this.

❖ I really don't want to tell anyone how I feel.

❖ My cigarettes are my vitamins.

❖ If my friends only knew what a mess I am.

MUSIC SELECTION

"Damn, It's Good to Be Me," Uncle Kracker

"The Joker/Everything I Own," sung by Jason Mraz and Christie
Hynde from Happy Feet

"Live," Lenny Kravitz

"The Heart of Life," John Mayer

"Wreckless Love," Alicia Keyes

ESSENTIAL OIL RECOMMENDATIONS

Cypress: Eases the feeling of loss and creates a sense of security and
grounding.

Patchouli: A relaxant that clarifies thoughts, allowing the discarding
of jealousies, obsessions, and insecurities.

Aroma Life: Energizes your life force and promotes heart vitality.

Gentle Baby: Comforting, soothing, relaxing, and beneficial
for reducing stress.

Sensation: Amplifies the excitement of experiencing new heights of
self-expression and awareness.

CHAPTER 3

Your Energetic System
Is Your Emotional System

"We are emotions and emotions are us; we cannot

separate emotions." – Dr. Candace Pert

THE EMOTIONAL CIRCLE OF LIFE
& THE FIVE VORTEXES OF EMOTION

Our emotional system is similar to nature; it's an all-inclusive system. Each emotion is related to all the other emotions, and every one of them is needed. This is aptly described in Chinese medicine's five-element system, which relates each of the five elements to a season and an emotion. Think of the five key emotions as a vortex of emotion, a vibrational field that affects the whole system. Together, they represent the emotional circle of life.

We'll begin with *grief*. We all grieve change. Grief represents letting go of the old – letting go of what was and beginning the process of preparing the way for the new. You can see how this operates in nature during fall. Fall is all about the leaves letting go and falling off the trees. They don't have to fight to let go; they just release. Some float on the ground and others swirl up in the air. Fall has much to teach us about respecting the process of release. As Dr. Christiane Northrup says:

> *"Grieving for the life you no longer have is power... you will never get from who you are now to who you want to be until you are willing to go through the process of grieving the life you thought you were going to have."*[19]

Next comes *fear*, which is about allowing yourself to go within. Fear follows grief because we're afraid of loss. Sometimes we harbor a fear that nothing will ever change, yet below the surface everything is preparing for new growth. Deepak Chopra calls this "the period of Divine Discontent." We need time for rest and reflection, and winter is that time. We observe how everything goes dormant on the surface. Our job is to feel the fear and allow calm and courage to manifest in the face of it. We forget that fear is a natural part of life. Because we don't want to look at it, we deny or bury it. This causes us to fear our feeling of fear, and we get stuck and don't even know it. Instead, you want to create a situation where you can incubate so you can get to insight. This allows you to put your insight into action when you move into spring.

The next emotion is *anger*. We are often taught that anger is wrong, yet in fact it actually serves us. Anger serves us best when we use it as motivation for focused creative action. As Maya Angelou says about anger:

"Use that anger, yes, you write it, you paint it, you dance it, you march it, you vote it, you do everything about it, you talk it... never stop talking about it." [20]

The expression of anger is needed, but don't throw it at anyone – including yourself. This might be how anger got such a bad wrap –we've thrown it more than used it as motivation for creative action. An anger that is focused allows us to discover solutions that lead to the next emotion, *joy*.

When we're in joy, we allow our hearts to connect in laughter, tears, clapping, or dancing – there are so many expressions that depict this emotion. Joy is summertime, when we celebrate and come together with others, feeling inspired by our connections. Some of the best childhood memories for most of us are the carefree days of summer. It's playing, enjoying the warmth, barbecues with friends, long days, and relaxing vacations. Summer is a celebration of being alive, and everything is in balance.

The final emotion on the emotional circle of life is *empathy*. In terms of the seasons, this corresponds with late summer. In ancient Italy, this was celebrated as the end of the main agricultural season, carried out each year on the 15th of August. Horses and other animals were given the day off and were decorated with flowers. Today, *Ferragosto* is still celebrated throughout Italy as a time to be with friends at the beach. It's the time of abundance, when we reap the harvest, the rewards of our growth. In nature, this is when we harvest the crops.

This abundance is where you discern the giving and caring for others. When you feel fully abundant yourself, you know what to keep to nourish yourself and what to give to others. You feel steady. Empathy provides the motivation for giving to yourself and others. Without empathy, you don't see the need for any type of nurturing. You're not aware of the need to have this balance of self-focused and outward nurturing that is required during this season.

We're all used to how the seasons naturally flow from one to the other. Although we don't like it at times, we accept the fact that seasonal change is a natural part of the rhythm of life. However, when it comes to our emotions, we have trouble recognizing the natural rhythmic flow that is just as real as the seasons. The ideal is to move through your emotions with balance and harmony. When you have balance and harmony simultaneously, you move through change with ease. Everything in life is in various states of change.

Our emotions let us know when we're resisting and we're flowing. When you're moving to the outer edges of this diagram, this is the place of the heart. It's from the heart that we respond to life's changes. If you find yourself in the emotions closer to the center (human experience), you're usually reacting unconsciously to what is occurring. When you find yourself in an emotional state, look at which of the five vortexes of emotion you're in, and then look for the positive expression of that vortex on the outer circle to lead you to the next step.

Emotion Is the Lynchpin

Emotion is the lynchpin in your system. It is the place where you can release. A lynchpin is defined as "a central cohesive source of support and stability." "Faith is his anchor," "The keystone of campaign reform was the ban on soft money," "He is the lynchpin of this firm," etc. Synonyms are anchor, mainstay, keystone, backbone. The lynchpin is the link to the mind, body, and spirit connection. This lynchpin is your emotional safety valve.

Think of your emotions as a place where you can blow off steam. This is why there truly are no negative emotions. Some emotions are a long way from the place you want to be hanging out, in the sense that you want to spend most of your time hanging out in what we typically call the positive emotions: love, joy, and peace. Because of this, there must be safety valves in the system, just like you have safety valves in your home's electrical system. Your electrical system requires a place where the breaker gets blown when the electricity goes through too fast. Your emotional system is an electromagnetic system, and power rushes through it, generated from your thoughts. Let's say you find yourself thinking negative or unpleasant thoughts, or criticizing, blaming, or judging yourself. When any of these thoughts get rocking and rolling, there has to be somewhere where to release them, to let them out – hence the need for the safety valve.

All emotions are an expression of where you are in the moment. It is important to actually allow yourself to have these safety valves. If you don't, your emotions build up and you have to find a place to store them within your body. This is how you freeze your emotions and wall off that part of you internally.

The best analogy we can think of is an office building with cubicles. When something happens that rattles you, you might lock those emotions away in one of your cubicles. Then something else happens, and you think, "Oh, I should not be having that emotion," and so you send that that one away to its appropriate cubicle, and on and on, until ultimately you have locked away half of your system. You have now minimized your very capacity to feel, because you have created all those places where you say, "I can't allow myself to feel that," or "I can't allow myself to feel this." It's amazing to observe that some people even do this with so-called positive emotions – they will not allow themselves to feel excessive joy, happiness, or peace, so those get walled off too.

We see a good example of this in the movie *As Good as It Gets*.[21] Melvin Udall (Jack Nicholson) is a writer who has cut himself off from the world. He's a terrific example of what happens when you don't allow emotion to flow in your life or allow yourself to connect with others. Melvin's emotional options are limited, and it's humorous to see how this affects him.

At times, we all have a narrow set of emotions we're willing to experience. Remember, we talked about your set point, and how your norm is around whatever that set point is. Many of us wall off these other places. These set points can be a narrow band of emotion that limits how much you allow yourself to feel. You only recognize sadness or anger when they are intense, instead of feeling the complete range of what your system has been built to do. Understand that these emotions are both a safety valve and a source of that marker to understand where you are in the moment. All of your emotions serve you. They help you understand yourself and the ways that you settle into various grooves.

Your emotions help you understand your way of responding to situations. Ideally, you'll get to a point where you see that all of your feelings are serving you. You know that they are serving you because it is happening, because you are experiencing it. Even when you are in the so-called darker moments, even when you are experiencing the emotion of rage, see if you can be still, look at it, and say, "Oh, my body is just releasing or just needs a place to allow that energy to flow out." Remember, energy follows thought, and when you've built up a head of steam you now have to allow a place to release it.

It is not unlike a pressure cooker. The steam has to come out somewhere. It either can be walled off in the body, or it can be allowed to release. It is your choice as to which way you want to go. However, if you keep storing it in the body, in your physical container, the ultimate impact will be that it gets transmuted into something else. You are using up all your energy, in a sense, to keep those emotions locked behind closed doors or cubicles not being accessed. We want you to understand that whatever you are feeling is absolutely serving you, and it is time for you to acknowledge what you are feeling so you can see where you are on the scale.

Feel Your Emotions but Don't Throw Them at Others

Feeling all of your emotions doesn't mean you have the right to "throw" them at others. That is not the goal. Feeling all your emotions is a way to recognize what is happening in you, what beliefs are being stirred up, and what you need to be addressing. It's a way of gaining more awareness of self and staying more present in the now. This allows you to start being grateful for all the things that are happening in your world – even in that moment of despair, that moment of anger. This way, you can almost simultaneously move to the thought, "Oh, I'm grateful for this!"

Instead, what we are inclined to do as human beings is constantly be angry when we are feeling those emotions. Instead of being able to look at a situation as something that is serving you, you actually want to be upset about the fact that you are feeling that emotion. So now you are actually sending yourself back down the road in the wrong direction. In other words, you are pushing yourself further into the storm, instead of allowing yourself to come into the light and be in the place where you can express gratitude that whatever is happening is cleaning out one of those locked cupboards internally. Or you might be grateful to recognize that you're not allowing an emotion to be real instead of allowing yourself to feel what you're feeling.

Emotion Is the Safety Valve for Your Energetic System

Think of your whole emotional system as a totality. Everything is related, similar to the body. Emotion is the lynchpin to the whole system because everything is interconnected and interrelated. Your emotions let you see how your body, mind, and soul are responding. Your emotions link your mind, body, and soul. They are a very tangible way to recognize what is going on with your whole person.

Your Higher Self, or Spirit, is the part of you that is part of God. Spirit is referred to by different names in each tradition, such as the Buddha nature, Christ-consciousness, Purusha, Allah, etc. This part of you never changes and is the source of all creation. When you allow this energy to flow through you, this part of you that is truly spirit revitalizes your soul, and that gets reflected out in your thinking and your physical body. Until you allow that energy through that is spirit, you can't revitalize your soul. You're stuck with the energy as it is. This is how your soul learns and develops.

The soul, mind, and body are the inputs, and the emotions are the outputs. Your energetic system is another name for your emotional system, because emotion is a condensed representation of what is going on. You might say, "I have to look at my thoughts; I have to discern my what my gut feeling is, or what is going on in my gut." When you think in terms of how your body is responding, how your mind is responding, you have to think about how your spirit is responding. Your emotions give you a condensed way of looking at that, because it represents the totality of that response.

We are not generally aware that our emotions are continually providing this level of sophisticated information. It's the ultimate canary in the mine, because you're getting multidimensional feedback. Your emotions could be giving you feedback on any one of these levels. It's as if your emotions are the output coming from any of the levels of mind, body, or spirit at any given time. It's like getting medical readouts from your physical system, your mental system, and your spiritual system – they all converge in your emotions. From that standpoint, your energetic system *is* your emotional system. It is a wonderful way to condense that output.

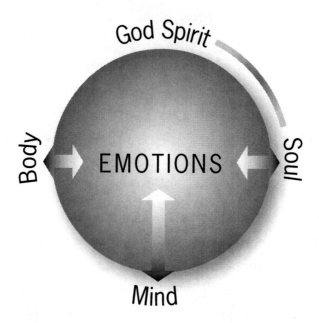

We say the emotions are the lynchpins because everything is interrelated. Think about the your system as a totality (i.e., "the hip bone is connected to the thigh bone"). The whole system is interconnected. The emotions are a very tangible way to recognize what is going on with your mind, body, and soul. That's what we mean by the lynchpin. When you see your emotion in the context of the lynchpin, you then create the opportunity for right action.

Your Emotions Serve Your Instincts and Intuition

When you are aware that emotion is this powerful lynchpin, you can start to see how your emotions enhance your instincts and intuition. They become a powerful guidance system that serves you.

In the Fox TV series *Lie to Me*,[22] Cal Lightman has created a successful company using his heightened instinctual skills. Lightman's clients come to him for help to determiine who's lying and who's telling the truth. The Lightman Group specializes in reading people's facial expressions to determine what emotions they are displaying. Lightman is an expert at reading people, and his staff is also highly skilled. With each episode Lightman or his team members utilize their instincts to solve cases.

In the "Honey" episode, Eric Matheson has been charged with killing his wife, and he's running from the police. Matheson takes Cal as a hostage to get his help to prove that he didn't kill his wife. He has a past with the police and knows he won't be treated fairly. Matheson is highly reactive, out of control. Lightman is clever; he takes his time and doesn't get reactive. He doesn't try to muscle the situation and quickly starts coming up with options that lead the gunman away from his staff. Cal Lightman studied with medicine men and native people all over the world, where he learned how to refine his instincts and trust his intuition. In this episode, we see how his instincts not only protect him and his staff but also help him to discover a solution that serves all involved.

Lightman's colleague, FBI agent Ben Reynolds, has his own instincts. We see how his field experience as an agent guides him in this high-stress situation. The remaining members of Lightman's staff utilize their intuition and, as a team, they swiftly come up with options that calm the situation. Because each of them could call on their intuition, they are able to discern truth and save lives.

We discount what our emotions are telling us and as a result, don't see how powerfully they serve us, and thus we miss the signs. "What... many others want to dismiss as a coincidence or a gut feeling is in fact a cognitive process, faster than we recognize and far different from the familiar step-by-step thinking we rely on so willingly,"[23] as Gavin De Becker says in *The Gift of Fear.*

How Do I Recognize My Intuition?

There are many ways intuition and instincts guide us. Some people get goose bumps (or GBS – Goose Bump Surplus, as members of the band Journey called it when they found a replacement lead singer). Some people have a heightened sense of smell – roses, mustiness, or fear and tension coming from perspiration and body odor. These smells guide them. For still others, the hair on the back of their neck sticks up. And we've all heard of "gut feeling." If you get any of these physical sensations, pay attention; you're getting valuable feedback, and if you read it correctly it can greatly serve you and others. If you don't currently recognize this amazing feedback system, perhaps you've blocked off your emotions without being aware of it.

How Do I Know That I've Blocked Off My Emotions?

Watch your thoughts, and as soon as you have any emotion, notice what happens in your body. Does it automatically tense up? Does it automatically physically or metaphorically take a step back? Do you mentally go to a place where you think, "I should not be feeling this"? This is often evident in those whose intent is to be spiritually evolved or who practice a strong faith and belief in God. Because they intend to be spiritual, some of their emotions may not fit these beliefs. For example, some believe it's not spiritual to be angry at someone, so they immediately try to lock it down. If there are some emotions that don't fit your spiritual beliefs, this can be an indicator that you have a place that is locked up. You'll recognize this when you think that some emotions are not okay and you can't feel what you are truly feeling. In other words, you have a judgment about it and immediately start criticizing yourself. As a result, you lock it back down again.

Emotion Is Your Compass and Feeds Your Perception

You want to access your full range of emotions at all times. If you do not allow yourself to have the full range of emotions, you are actually denying the full capability of the system you have available to you. Think of a compass. Would you ask a compass not to show you north or south? A compass that can't give accurate directions is of little use. It doesn't give you a pointer or marker of where you are. When you try to shut down what you are feeling, you are actually stopping your compass. It's as if you are saying, "North and south are not valid – I'll only look at east and west." The more you shut your compass down, the more lost you become. You're in an internal fog and don't know which way to turn.

The Mind and the Time of Reason

In our society, in this time and place in history, reason is valued above all. Because this age of reason has dominated our culture, most of us source only the mind for discernment and the decisions we make. We don't normally seek answers from our spiritual feelings, what we choose to feel, or how our body is reacting. We put so much importance on our thinking that we've lost touch with our powerful emotional compass. We rationalize everything, and this limits our guidance.

In the movie *The Squid and the Whale*,[24] Bernard Berkman (Jeff Daniels) lives in his head. He's emotionally detached and has built a wall around himself with his intellect and his use of vocabulary. The only emotion available to him is anger. Throughout the movie, we see how his reactive anger clouds his judgment and keeps him stuck while trying to discover rational solutions to his problems.

Bernard is going through a divorce with his wife, Joan (Laura Linney). Understandably, this change is an emotional experience for Bernard, especially because it's beyond his ability to rationalize it. Because he has relied so much on his intellectual abilities, he struggles to digest this emotional experience. He wants to shut down and think his way through it. He loses touch with his feelings, and this stirs up the reactivity. Bernard wants to rationalize everything. Even at the end of the movie, Bernard doesn't get it and rationalizes his heart attack as simply being tired.

Your Emotions Are the Source of Creativity

You have more creativity in your life experiences when the expression of your emotions has free range, including their intensity. On the emotional continuum, you have a range from negative six to positive six, but you also have the depth of the groove. Think of the intensity as the indicator of the depth of the groove.

Many great artists are actually accessing places of heaviness or despair. Their art expresses these emotions in a deeper and intense way through anger or sadness. But think about what it creates in terms of expression – it's just as valid as great joy and gives others permission to express their emotions too. For example, think of Carl Orff's opera, *Carmine Burana*,[25] and his famous piece "O Fortuna," which today is used throughout popular culture. This intense piece depicts humans as helpless victims subject to the great wheel of fortune. Our emotions are stirred by this music, yet most of us don't know the despair, anger, and railing against fate it was intended to express. That doesn't prevent us from using this piece to sell cars, promote movies, and even market beer. We love how it expresses that it's okay to feel all the emotions and their intensity. When you can access this full range along with its intensity, your creativity expands to new levels.

All The Emotions Are Serving – The Full Range

There isn't a specific emotion that needs to be cut out. As you can see above, even despair has a purpose. Despair means that you have blocked out the light. When you recognize this, it's time for you to allow yourself to open up that light a little bit. In other words, it's time to help yourself feel a little better in that moment. Orff's expression of despair created something entirely new that's still relevant today.

What About Leaders — How Does Emotion Impact Their Role?

When a leader in any organization can access the full range of emotion, they have more capacity for empathy towards their team and an enhanced perception of what is truly going on. They become more aware of the cues their body is giving them and can come up with creative solutions to problems. The purpose of this emotional awareness is internal guidance; it's not meant to be thrown at others. This guidance heightens a leader's perception of what they are being told and how it is being delivered. If you have the capacity to experience and understand the whole range of emotion within you, then you can discern if you are getting a gut response or if someone is just reacting. You can ask yourself, "Was there a thought that got impeded there? Am I reacting to it, or am I discerning?" You also have more empathy to help lead others when they get stuck. The better you get at this, the more you trust your emotions and your gut reactions.

Differences between Men and Women

Typically speaking, women usually allow themselves to feel their full range of emotion more than men. Women are accustomed to dealing with young children, and children show us how to do this beautifully. They are open to the full range of emotions and allow themselves to go there. One minute they are screaming, and the next they can be joyful and in bliss.

How Do I Know if I'm Reacting or Responding?

In the beginning of this chapter, we talked about our diagram called the Emotional Circle of Life. We mentioned that the emotions closer to the center are ones of a reactive nature. Experiencing these emotions can make you feel as if you don't have a choice – this emotional expression is just what happens. This type of reactivity is a normal human experience, but even though it seems normal to react, it causes unforeseen problems. The very nature of reactivity is that it's unconscious and can get out of hand. Reaction makes all of us blind; we become unable to see others or consider their feelings.

We describe the outer edge of the diagram as the vortexes of emotion: grief, fear, anger, joy, and empathy. These emotions can help you respond to situations in empowering ways, to choose and be aware. They tend to have similar changes to our systems as the seasons do to nature. These emotions also can be reactive when they are unconscious. However, when you're aware of the empowering nature of these vortexes of emotion, you respond in ways that get you back to joy. With practice, you get back to joy faster and faster.

We've created a chart to show the empowering aspects of response vs. the disempowering impacts of reactivity. We call this the Foundation of Emotional Understanding.

FOUNDATION OF EMOTIONAL UNDERSTANDING
REACTIVITY vs RESPONSE

Conscious   CHOICE   Conscious

**RESPONSE —
PEACEFUL ACTION**

REACTIVITY

Unconscious   NO CHOICE   Unconscious

Responsiveness is on the top, and reactivity is on the bottom. When you go unconscious, you are in reactivity, and when you become more conscious of your reactivity, you come up to responsiveness. Response is the place where you can choose. Response is the path to choice and freedom. As consciousness diminishes, you drop into reactivity, which takes away your choice.

When you're reacting, you normally don't realize what is going on – you just feel out of control. When reactivity gets less and less, you get to a point where your consciousness can elevate. At one end, you can raise your consciousness about becoming reactive until you get to a point that you can respond. When you travel the road of response, response, response, you reach a point where you are not thinking any more – and that is not truly responding. It is an unconscious responding that leads you to slip back into reactivity. On the reactivity scale, you can become less unconscious until you reach the awareness that you have a choice in responding. You want to create a strong foundation in your life. Just like a building structure, the square is a solid foundation. It is the Foundation of Emotional Understanding.

Emotional reactivity deepens the grooves. If you are deepening the groove, you just make it harder for yourself to respond in the future. As you deepen the groove, it's like driving at a fast speed and hitting a brick wall. As you get stronger and stronger reactions, you eventually come to a place where you will stop yourself dead in your tracks.

We sometimes think there is an upside to our emotional reactivity. We think that this now allows us to express how we feel, and we believe we're justified throwing it at a person. We get to tell them how we feel, and it becomes someone else's fault, not our own. While it is true that we are meant to express how we feel, we don't get to throw it others. You must, in a sense, be very clear about how *you* feel and recognize that nobody else has created that feeling in you. If you're the one reacting, it's usually your stuff to look at and nobody else's fault.

Cultural Irony

We expect people to react without being emotional. Our society has a double standard: we are not supposed to react in the sense that we're supposed to be in control. When a person does not react in certain ways under certain situations, that individual is considered cold and callous. Think about examples of people testifying in court who have been accused of some horrendous crime. We watch them to see if they are remorseful; we expect this reaction – it's almost a requirement. We have come to expect that if others are not reacting, they don't care. This creates a dichotomy: we want people to react, but they are not supposed to be emotional. No wonder we get confused! We spend a great deal of time judging our own reactivity and that of others. What's the point of judging your reactivity? Look how confusing the signals are. No two people react in the same fashion, regardless of the situation. All reactions are as different and unique as fingerprints.

Your Change and Development Can Make Others Reactive

Emotional reactivity in ourselves and those around us has a cost. It limits our ability to choose differently. When you begin making your needs a priority, it can create reactivity in others. You're no longer predictable emotionally, and your new inner strength can be unsettling. When we are anxious about how others will react, we don't pursue our needs because we're afraid of getting their reactivity thrown at us. It's just easier to keep pleasing others. This is especially true when dealing with an employer, a spouse, a parent, or any other person we perceive as having influential power.

As we've already said, reactivity has become so common that we're uncomfortable when someone doesn't have an expected reaction. It's as if they don't care or are coldly responding in the face of a situation that demands emotional reactivity. Somehow reactivity has come to mean that you care because you're uncontrollably upset.

Because we've become so accustomed to our own reactive nature, we can't see how often we take what people say and do personally. When you take other people's emotional reactivity personally, you are handing over your freedom to them. Their approval becomes the most important thing – far more important than what *you* want or how *you* want to live *your* life. You're no longer free to see how you really feel about a situation. You are reacting to the perceived control the other person is exerting. When someone is reactive and spraying you with their emotions, it's usually an indication of how *they're* feeling and truly has nothing to do with *you*.

You might be thinking, "If I don't react, then others will walk all over me... I have to react to keep my ground and earn respect." This widespread belief just creates more reactivity, and the reactive volley perpetuates. As Byron Katie says, "Defense is the first act of war." There's no peace to be found in defensively reacting to the emotions thrown at you by others. You'll just perpetuate the "reactive war," and you certainly won't find peace.

In Dr. Martin Luther King, Jr.'s autobiography[26], he tells a story about driving from Atlanta to Chattanooga, Tennessee, with his brother Alfred. The oncoming drivers were forgetting to dim their lights as they passed on the highway. As a result, the high beams were blinding; it was a discourteous thing to do. Alfred said, "I'm tired of this now, and when the next car that comes by here and refuses to dim their lights, I'm going to refuse to dim mine." Don't we all feel that way when others are emotionally reacting towards us? We want to flash our high beams right back in their face to get them to back down. Dr. King responded, "Somebody has to have some sense on this highway; if somebody doesn't have sense enough to dim the lights, we'll all end up destroyed." Emotional reactivity can be just as blinding as this high-beam example on the highway, especially when we take it personally.

Frozen Emotion Needs to Thaw

Sometimes emotional reactivity makes a person want to shut down and withdraw. Just the thought of getting sprayed with more reactivity causes some of us to stuff our emotions. It's as if we put them in the freezer to be addressed later. We certainly won't let the reactive people around us know how we feel; we'll merely get more emotions thrown our way. Maintaining this type of control over your own deep feelings is a way to protect yourself, but it can feel suffocating. It often leads to avoiding necessary discussions, a loss of personal boundaries, and a pattern of trying to please reactive individuals so you don't feel their discomfort.

Depending on your family or cultural norms, stuffing your emotions can be the proper way to behave; there might be great pressure to prevent you from allowing your emotions to flow. When you freeze your emotions long enough, however, it can be hard to get in touch with how you really feel, and this creates another set of challenges.

In the movie *The King's Speech,*[27] we have an example of how to stay grounded emotionally while allowing another to thaw his emotions. Lionel Logue (Geoffrey Rush) is a highly skilled speech therapist who is introduced to a famous and powerful new client, the future King George VI (Colin Firth). Lionel has the challenging task of helping his client work with his stammering. King George, or "Bertie" as Lionel calls him, doesn't feel fit to be king. Bertie believes his stammering is an embarrassment to him, his family, and his country. Lionel helps Bertie to begin thawing his emotions and provides a space where it's okay for his past pain and struggles to be released. Lionel has much practice in this work. He has worked with many men returning from war who have experienced trauma. Lionel helped these men by allowing their emotions to be expressed and their psyches to heal.

Bertie experienced a difficult childhood. He was ridiculed for his stammering, and it seems he was neglected as a child. We see how these experiences have remained with him and how he stuffed all his emotion.

Lionel shows us how to stay calm and centered in the face of someone releasing their frozen emotions. He doesn't become reactive, and he does not take the King's emotional responses personally. Lionel becomes a powerful example of how to respond to others instead of react. It takes calm strength and gentle courage to remain balanced in the face of emotional releasing.

How Do I Know If I'm Reacting or Releasing?

It can be tricky and complicated to recognize when you're unconsciously reacting and when you're releasing. Here are some general tips we've experienced that might help you. Reactivity often has a recognizable pattern: Person A does something and Person B reacts. This reaction typically happens regardless of who is involved. The content is very similar and produces the same reaction. You start to see a pattern; you begin to hear yourself complaining about the same thing repeatedly.

Releasing is more difficult to detect. We've found that releasing looks like overblown emotion that is disproportionate to the issue at hand. It's similar to an explosion that comes out of nowhere, and it has an intensity that's just not rational. Think of a volcano erupting without warning. Bertie shows us examples of what this looks like. He starts to release his emotions with much power during discussions of his past. Each time he explodes, he feels better and has less of an emotional charge around his stammering. Bertie has kept all these emotions locked up inside, and they erupt with great force when the pressure is released.

When you recognize that you're releasing, it's beneficial to seek out an experienced practitioner, clergy member, or teacher. Many times, we unconsciously expect our mate, family, or friends to play the counselor role. This can be asking too much of them, especially if their pattern is to react unconsciously. It's not their job to facilitate you through these times. They can certainly be supportive, but too much releasing can put unnecessary stress on your most cherished connections. Bertie didn't expect his wife to counsel him through these challenging moments. Having Lionel's expertise allowed her to lovingly support him to keep going.

Remember, this can be challenging work, so get some help and know that you're worth it. The more your emotion builds up, the more problems you'll experience later. Sue-Anne uses the example of defrosting a freezer with her clients. It takes time to melt the layers of ice, and you can't force it without damaging the freezer. A skilled practitioner can help you to melt your frozen emotions, and this will make the process much smoother. Bertie was fortunate to have such a skilled teacher in Lionel, and he ends up gaining a lifelong friend.

We recommend viewing *The King's Speech.* As you watch it, here are some things to consider:

❖ How did Bertie's emotions become so frozen?

❖ How do you freeze your emotions?

Intensity Can Get in the Way of Both Response and Reactivity

Response leads to choice, which can also lead to more reactivity. Think about a new goal you have chosen. That goal may be to lose weight, so you plan to take up exercise, which is a good response to this goal. You decide to exercise five hours a day, even though you have not exercised at all in the last several years. A response of five hours a day, even though it's a positive response, is intense and too extreme. As a result, you will most likely cause damage to your body.

Responses need to be considered choices, not unconscious reactivity. You don't want to create another groove. You could end up using a sledgehammer for something that does not require this level of power. An example of this is the way we overmedicate ourselves. We have a sniffle, and we decide to throw everything at it, including antibiotics. You are taking action in the sense that this is a positive response; it's not just a reaction. However, if it becomes totally unconscious, it has indeed become another reaction. Now you have lost your ability to choose. You are living in a closed system. Everything circles back. You are unable to make an effect in one area without affecting another (e.g., the butterfly effect).

If you know yourself, you'll be more likely to catch yourself before reactivity sets in, and you will be able to respond in a way that fits you, such as turning to empathy. If anger gets out of control, you have no empathy. When someone is reacting, listen to the background story. This is the place where you can gain a deeper understanding, and it can lead you to compassion. Reaction is unconscious, and many times it is based in fear; response is conscious and can originate from love or other higher emotions.

Own Your Own Reactivity

If you're the one reacting, you are accountable for the emotion, not the person or event that prompted your reactivity. That doesn't mean there isn't an issue to be addressed; there's something for everyone involved to discover.

When you catch yourself, we suggest you put yourself in timeout. Work through it without throwing it at somebody. The ideal is to re-center yourself quicker and quicker. The more you practice, the better you'll get, and the more peace you'll realize.

In Mirabai Starr's book, *St. Francis of Assisi*, she speaks about Francis' ability to always return to peace. "It is comforting to discover that Francis of Assisi suffered and lamented, lost his temper and forfeited his dignity, rebelled against the rebels and lashed out at the meek. That, like us, he fell again and again. And that he continued to stand up, brush himself off, and recommit his life to God."[28]

Emotions Open Us to Grace

Many of us resist change and rail against it. We struggle with letting go and dig ourselves deeper and deeper in a groove of anger or grief, which keeps us from joy and from receiving divine grace.

Be the observer of your emotions so you can allow grace to come in. Grace lifts you above cause and effect. Grace lifts you above this duality; it takes you out of the realm of *doing* to a place of *receiving* God's blessings. Grace allows you to feel forgiveness; the score no longer needs to be evened. Grace comes from your ability to detach from what is happening in your world. When you come to a place of discernment, if you are detached while discerning, you allow grace.

The movie *My Sister's Keeper*[29] is a story about the Fitzgerald sisters, whose lives are focused on doing whatever it takes to keep the eldest sister, Kate, alive. Kate (Sofia Vassilieva) has a terminal illness; she's dying from cancer of the blood and bone marrow. Her sister Anna (Abigail Breslin) was conceived with the intent of providing Kate with the needed blood to help save Kate's life. Their mother, Sara (Cameron Diaz), is reactively protective of Kate. Her focus is only on beating this illness and saving Kate's life. She neglects everyone else in the family, including herself.

Sara struggles to keep Kate alive, while Anna and Kate come up with a way to allow her to let go and surrender to her illness. This emotional journey eventually brings both Kate and her mother to a place of surrender and acceptance. They let go of resistance and their grief is allowed to express itself. The grief melts the protective barriers between them, and a type of opening occurs. It's in this experience that Sara and Kate receive a blessing, a type of grace that gives meaning to their emotional experience.

"Grace is openness. It is the spiritual strength and the intuitive vision that you can experience while performing an action. While remaining open to a particular situation, you are letting go of your ego and narrow-minded views. This transforms your mind into a better channel through which divine energy can flow. That flow of divine energy and its expression through our actions is grace."[30] ◈

❈ CHAPTER SUMMARY ❈

You now see the powerful guidance systems your emotions provide. They are truly the unsung heroes of your energetic system. When you allow yourself to flow emotionally, you gain deeper intuition, you flow through change more easily, and your emotions help you recognize what is truly going on. When you can see emotion as the lynchpin of the mind, body, and soul, you are able to understand what it's telling you. You can catch yourself when you're reactive and quickly move to a response that empowers you and others. When you become a master of understanding your emotions, you truly know how your energetic system works. Now you are able to use your emotions in the most effective way.

BELIEF STATEMENTS REPRESENTED IN THIS CHAPTER:

Energizing Beliefs

- ❖ It's not my fault when my parents don't get along.

- ❖ My judgments have an impact on my family.

- ❖ I never allow my children to be pawns between my mate and I.

- ❖ I don't perpetuate power struggles within my family.

- ❖ My children are still young and need my love and guidance.

- ❖ I retain my own voice.

- ❖ I relate to my children where they are.

- ❖ Vulnerability is strength.

- ❖ I like a mate that brings his or her emotion to our bedroom.

De-Energizing Beliefs

❖ I take sides within my family and defend them at all costs.

❖ I have to respond when I'm challenged so I can save face.

❖ I idolize my parents and forget they're just human like me.

❖ It's not safe for me to be vulnerable with my mate.

❖ I can intellectualize myself through any of my problems.

❖ My mate can never make up his/her mind.

❖ I gain prestige by portraying myself as all knowing, and I make up stories to maintain that image.

❖ I don't feel good about myself, so I try to win anywhere I can.

❖ I expect my students and children to go beyond me.

❖ I tell myself and the world lies about my accomplishments.

❖ I let my rational lies run my life.

❖ How others behave establishes how I feel.

❖ Being seen as emotional is a sign of weakness for a man.

❖ If I show my emotional side as a man, I'll look like a fool.

❖ My man has to be an emotionally strong man.

❖ I can't be emotionally vulnerable in my marriage and in our bedroom.

MUSIC SELECTION

Liederkreis – Robert Schumann: "Ich Wandelte Unter Den Bäumen,"

"Ring Shout... Peace of Mind," Winton Marsalis

"La Contestacion," Los Lonely Boys

"If French Fries Were Fat-Free," Alan Jackson

"Above Ground," Norah Jones

ESSENTIAL OIL RECOMMENDATION

Clary Sage: Enhances one's ability to dream and is very calming and stress-relieving.

Jasmine: Uplifting; counteracts hopelessness, nervous exhaustion, anxiety, depression, indifference, and listlessness.

Roman Chamomile: Calming, relaxing properties; has been traditionally used to soothe muscle spasms.

Envision: Renews faith in the future, stimulates creative and intuitive abilities, and amplifies emotional fortitude to achieve your goals and dreams.

Present Time: An empowering fragrance that creates a feeling of being in the moment; helps you to get beyond the past so you can move forward.

CHAPTER 4

This Is Perfect—How Do I Know? Because It's Happening!

"Where we already are is the path and the goal" – Jack Kornfield

We all, at one time or another, get caught in the trap of grasping for the perfect job, the perfect house, the perfect body, the perfect companion, and we focus on how perfect life will be when we get more money or retire, etc. It's grasping for a perfection that is outside of us that can trip us up if we're not aware of it. Nothing in the external is perfect per se because it's always changing. So how then can something be perfect because it's happening? It's the process of life we're referring to, not some external achievement.

We can look at the process of nature and notice how the seasons are always perfect. When we're in the middle of winter and tired of being cold and gray, we never doubt that spring will eventually arrive. We know this seasonal process is perfect and always works out fine. However, we can still trip ourselves up if we get stuck in a seasonal event (a flood, a hurricane, a tornado) and think that maybe nature shouldn't be this way. In this respect, we're not referring to individual events in our lives; we are really talking about seeing how the *process* is perfect. Individual events serve us in ways we'll discuss in the next chapter. It's when we can see the world and our lives as a process – without our judgments, projections, and assumptions – that we can discover how that process serves and is perfect.

The seasons help us to see that there is an intrinsic harmony all around us, and when we can flow with it, we have more joy in our lives. Ancient cultures were aware of nature's harmony and became skilled at living in tune with it. As technology has progressed, we've lost sight of nature's perfect process and how to stay connected with it harmoniously. Technological advancement is a wonderful thing, yet we are still learning to balance this with love and respect for our natural environment. This is why we are only now realizing the impact technology has had on our environment. The so-called green movement is trying to implement new processes to once again be in harmony with nature. While at this time this evolution can be met with resistance, it's just another reminder of the permanence that change has on all of life. Nature always has a way to correct itself, and when we recognize this and are in harmony with it, we'll discover outcomes that by hindsight may look perfect. It's from this macro view that we can see the perfect process being played out. When we try to find perfection in what is happening now and then rail against it, we lose this understanding of harmony.

How does this apply to our lives? Each of us are on our own journey that's leading us perfectly to what we intend for our lives. We sometimes lose sight of this – we resist change and try to grasp for something outside of us that we think will be perfect. It's as though we are hoping to arrive one day in "Perfectville, USA," where we will be happy forever. When you find yourself feeling this way, you may notice that it can get in the way of your happiness because you never feel like you're getting what you want. When we try to attain what we think will be a perfect life, we set ourselves up for heartbreak. The nature of life is change. As a result, perfection is always in flux and never stagnant, and that makes achieving perfection a fleeting goal. When we can't achieve it, we try to change ourselves so we can adhere to what others think is perfect instead of what feels right to us. Since we can't seem to achieve this "perfect" life, we think there must be something wrong with us, so we turn to more external solutions that we think will get us back on track. Trying to live a "perfect" life may require negating our feelings, and it can feel like we no longer have any freedom. Life becomes more complicated and difficult than it needs to be.

The seasons are like the phases of our lives. Do you expect it to be winter when it is spring? Each season has its own perfect serving. Many of us think we should always be in summer. It's become a Western way of life. We've accepted that the norm is being able to shop twenty-four hours a day, work without vacations, and constantly press for more action like the type taken in summer. The end of summer in Texas is what happens to you, and it's called burnout. Even the plants look wiped out and need a break. Then the harvest comes, and we take time to celebrate our hard work. Think of the Emotional Circle of Life chart in Chapter 3. The end of summer is the time to have empathy for ourselves, to steady and nurture ourselves for the work we participated in that provided the harvest.

Next, we move into letting go of what we no longer need and till the land. Activity in nature does slow down during winter, but our culture doesn't want any other season but spring, summer, and harvest. We've lost the awareness of the need for letting go, and going deep.

In the movie *Far from Heaven*,[31] we see a family in the 1950s living what looks like a perfect life. They have the perfect house, the perfect career, the perfect marriage, and obedient and loving children. It appears they have all the money they need. There's much effort that goes into keeping these external attributes on display for others to approve as examples of their perfect life. In many ways, we all unconsciously strive for this life and think then we'll be happy. This movie gives us an example of how trying to live a perfect life is far from perfect. It becomes rigid, and those that don't share our perspectives become our enemies. There's little freedom in this way of living, no one is allowed to be themselves, and few are truly happy. We then teach our children that this is the way to live, and it perpetuates with another generation.

When we're not focusing on living or creating the perfect life for ourselves, we look at the world around us and get disappointed when *it's* not perfect. Not only should our life be perfect, but now the world has to be perfect too. How could we ever have a world that's perfect for everybody? It's simply not possible.

In the movie *A Single Man*,[32] George (played by Colin Firth) is in deep grief over the loss of his longtime mate. He can't seem to move past it and doesn't want to live anymore. Director Tom Ford takes us through one of George's days, where he suddenly starts to notice the beauty of the smallest details that occur during these twenty-four hours. Tom Ford shows us perfect moments of beauty, color, and sounds. The more George notices these perfect moments, the more he recognizes them. He shows us that this is possible even while simultaneously being in a deep groove of grief. This movie gives us an example of "being in the moment." If we all could see this level of beauty in the moment, our lives would feel more and more perfect. When George starts to recognize this, he no longer wants to die.

Looking for these small details in the moment can be a practice that keeps us from grasping for some perfection that's yet to come. When we start to recognize more and more of these moments, we also begin to notice how synchronistic the process of life is. Sometimes we have to look back on our lives from 40,000 feet to begin to realize that being alive and experiencing the process of growing and learning can be perfect.

When we decided to write this book, our logical minds expected it to be a linear process. Sue-Anne had the title and the names of the chapters ready to go. She had been planning on writing this book for years. We figured we'd just start on Chapter 1 and go from there. We estimated this could all be wrapped up in about six months to a year. However, this was not the process that unfolded. It was more like building a house. Once the frame goes up, the other sections of the house come together as they do. This is how our process worked. One day we'd work on one chapter, and the next we'd be in an entirely different section without any clue why. Our minds wanted it to make logical sense; there were times when we were confused and didn't understand the process, although we kept going. Eventually, we recognized that working on emotions is not linear, so writing about emotions shouldn't be linear either. We use this example because it's analogous to our lives. Just like writing this book, we thought we needed all the answers up front, but we discovered that was a recipe for frustration and can be a disaster. Once we figured out that this process was serving us in a perfect way, we got better at flowing with it. Some days we did better than others. However, we can look back after three years of writing and see how it all worked out perfectly, serving us in the end.

Cultivate a Willingness to Change

There are some areas in our life we are just unwilling to address. We desire improvements in a particular area, but it has to be on our terms. If life would just go the way *I* want it to – now that sounds perfect, doesn't it? What we can't see is how much we get in the way of what we desire. We pray for change, just so long as it doesn't disrupt our job or our marriage. There are just some areas that are off-limits. This belief inhibits our ability to receive the guidance that comes our way. Change seems so scary. That's why we suggest starting by cultivating a willingness to change. This cultivation will prepare you for moments of clarity that perfectly guide you toward your desires.

In the movie *Liar Liar*,[33] Fletcher Reede (Jim Carrey), is a defense attorney who uses lying to manipulate his way through life. He's unable to see how this way of being has affected his son, his former wife, and his career. As a result, Fletcher has no idea what truth is for him in any area of his life. He doesn't know what he feels. When his five-year-old son's birthday wish comes true, Fletcher is unable to lie for a complete day. At first, he's not aware of what has happened to him, and he struggles to get through the day without being able to lie. It's humorous to see the messes this causes in his life.

We all go through similar communication experiences. Some people minimize communication and leave out vital details. Others want to share every detail, and their listeners get lost in the weeds. Eventually, there's a restructuring of the way we communicate, and this occurs for all of us on a regular basis. It looks messy, and it can be equally as frustrating as it was to Fletcher Reede. How can this benefit us in a perfect way? It can be a beneficial time for reflection and review to discover how you want to adapt to new rhythms. As you explore a different point of view, a new comprehension unfolds. When you recognize this happening in your life, seek to understand it; otherwise, you'll rely on your assumptions – which are often erroneous.

As Fletcher begins to realize that it was his son's wish that prevented him from lying, he starts to look at his life with different eyes and a new clarity. Only then can he see how lying has impacted his life and hurt others. He displays a willingness to change. This awareness becomes his perfect moment of truth and understanding, which allows him to discover what he truly desires for his life. He comes out of the fog, and there's a burst of clarity that perfectly guides him. Because he accepts the wish as real, he starts to work with being truthful, and this opens his heart to new desires. When perfect clarity happens to us, there's usually no turning back to the old ways of living. It's as if the proverbial Genie is out of the bottle and there's no putting her back in. You realize that life is better, and you aren't willing to go back, and that's the perfection in what has happened.

David's Clarity: Leaving Ford

When David was still at Ford, he cohosted a trip for dealers who had won a regional sales contest. The winners enjoyed a few days at Waterfall Alaska, a luxury fishing resort. The resort was on an island near Ketchikan, Alaska. The only way to get there was by floatplane. The entire group was immersed into intensely beautiful nature, and time seemed to slow down. There was only one phone on the island, which only worked intermittently. All there was to do was fish, sleep, eat, and drink. It was the first time in David's career where he slowed down and experienced moments of deep peace. One day, he heard the whales singing while fishing, and another day, he caught more fish than he ever imagined. The sound of the bald eagles was ever-present. He found himself standing in the rain, and he couldn't believe how pleasant it felt on his face. The air seemed sweeter, the food tasted better, and nature was never so beautiful. The peacefulness caught him by surprise, and the joy that followed was equally amazing.

As David was waiting on the dock, getting ready to leave, he started to think about how he didn't want to go back to the tension and stress he felt on his job. A yearning within started to build. He wanted to feel this peace more in his life. It was a scary yearning for freedom that he knew was problematic. In that moment, his boss and mentor leaned over to him and said, "You know you'll be in Detroit in a couple months... it's a done deal." This news would have brought him excitement and joy prior to the trip. But now, he knew something had to change. His Genie was out of the bottle, and she wasn't going back in. Yes, it was his moment of clarity, but it wasn't what he expected. David moved his family to Detroit, and Ford sent him back to Texas the following year. Within six months of his return to Texas, he knew it was time to leave Ford.

Sue-Anne' Clarity: US Citizenship

Sue-Anne initially moved to the US for love; she married an American she met while working in Australia. She had her green card, but she never thought citizenship was necessary. When her marriage didn't work out, she eventually returned to Australia. Before leaving the US, though, she a dated another man for a year. While they didn't click long-term, she and his teenaged daughter, Carissa, did. They quickly bonded and became friends.

Sue-Anne intended to settle in Sydney, near her family and friends. She had promised Carissa that she'd return for her high-school graduation. When she came to the US for the graduation, Sue-Anne experienced difficulty with US immigration. While everything was in order, the experience led her to believe she'd have more problems if Carissa ever needed her help. It was then that she realized citizenship was to be her priority. If she couldn't work in the US anymore, she wouldn't be there as backup for Carissa. However, the only way was to become a US citizen, which required a five-year mandatory stay – and this meant possibly losing her Australian citizenship. It was a big decision for Sue-Anne. She meditated on it and surrendered to God, asking for help, and then it became clear what she needed to do. With perfect clarity, Sue-Anne moved back to the US once again for love, and after five years became an American citizen.

Sue-Anne uprooted her life, not knowing if she'd ever get her Aussie citizenship again. She did indeed lose it temporarily, but eventually discovered a way to get it back. Sue-Anne had been so afraid that she wouldn't be able to go home – just the thought of not getting back was unthinkable. She remembers taking it to God and praying for help. Before her meeting with the Australian authorities, the *Oprah* show flashed on the screen in the immigration office. Right then, she knew everything would work out okay. Oprah was somebody that lived her life with faith and trusted where she was led. It was as if her warm aunt stopped by to encourage her.

The day that Sue-Anne flew back to the US, Australia returned her citizenship. She now enjoys dual-citizenship in both countries.

Be Aware of Your Own Self-Imposed Stereotypes

We limit ourselves and others when we cling to stereotypes. It doesn't matter whether it's politics, religion, family, nationality, finances, etc. – they can all become limiting. Every category comes with its own set of inherent and rigid rules. When you put yourself and others in these groupings, you limit all possibilities. Don't allow anyone to define you in any stereotype, and catch yourself when you try to define others. Stereotypes limit your life experiences and your opportunities to connect with others. Notice how you respond when someone asks you what you do, or what church you attend, or what school your children are in, etc. These become self-limiting identities.

In the movie *Down to Earth*,[34] Chris Rock plays Lance Burton, a stand-up comedian who gets a second shot at life as a wealthy white business tycoon. We watch how all these stereotypes play out for Lance and we observe the complexities inherent with his new opportunity to see life through different lenses.

This Is Perfect, Not Our Definition of Perfect

We often don't see the perfection of the events in our life until we have 20/20 hindsight. So many of us buy into the old adage, "I'll believe it when I see it." When you're looking for the inherent built-in perfection in your life, you have to believe it *before* you see it. You must believe that it is perfect *now*, even when you don't see it. This is the reason hindsight reveals the clarity – sometimes it's just difficult to see how the events of your life are serving you until you can look back and reflect. When you understand this, you can start to discover how occurrences that don't seem perfect actually serve you and usually were better for you than *your* definition of perfect. When you develop this understanding in the now moments of your life, you develop a growing acceptance that the flow of life is perfect. You begin to look for the gift in what's happening in the moment. This usually helps you move through the process much quicker, with less resistance, and with a spirit of expectancy.

Usually our interpretation of perfection is an established expectation. When our expectations are not realized, we lose sight of the perfection and are left frustrated. Think of how you feel when you expect a bus or an airplane to arrive at a certain time and it's late. You get irritated, don't you? Or you wanted to lose ten pounds in thirty days and you only lost five. We all can think of countless examples in our lives when our expectations weren't met and we weren't happy about it – and many times we were angry. We live in a time and culture where setting expectations and then achieving them is the formula for successful outcomes. We're told that we have to make those expectations happen and if we don't, we're not taking charge of our lives. It's as if we have to force our outcomes or they won't happen. We think that our established expectations guarantee perfect outcomes, and then we'll be happy. In effect, we set ourselves up for disappointment if that outcome doesn't come to fruition. Our possibilities are limited, and so are our outcomes.

As we look back, neither of us realized that we'd eventually meet, begin working together, and embark on writing this book. Both of our moment of clarity examples brought us back to Texas, living nine miles away from each other. We were perfectly guided to work with each other even though, at the time, neither one of us understood why. How could we have ever made this happen? We each had different expectations of what perfect looked like. But looking back, it truly was perfect.

"Life happens when you're busy making plans" – John Lennon, "Beautiful Boy"

Expectations Get in the Way

Expectation is a mental state when in you are in your head about what you expect. Whether good or bad, it doesn't make a difference – it's a closed system, and your mind is taking the lead and calling the shots. You're trying to make something or someone match your definition of perfect.

David's expectation was a successful career at Ford, and Sue-Anne expected that she'd be living in her beloved home of Sydney, Australia. Neither of us thought we'd be working together, writing books, and exploring new ways of living a peaceful life.

Does This Mean We Don't Set Any Goals We Can Work Toward Achieving?

A goal by its very nature has limits; it's usually on a time frame, with very specific metrics that must be met. It's more of a closed objective that most of us see as the requirement to success. It's not wrong to have goals, but there are simply limitations that can steal your peace when you don't meet those goals. We set goals to motivate ourselves, and we establish intentions that inspire us. Whereas expectancy allows for all possibilities without knowing the "how," goals are our expectations of "what" we do to keep us motivated.

Expectancy Is the State of Anticipating

Expectancy is the feeling or energy of optimism. Time isn't the leading factor in expectancy. A surfer that is waiting for the next wave is in expectancy. There's a knowing that a wave will eventually arrive. Expectancy is the place where you recognize the synchronistic events that are happening all around you. It's a place where you stay open and curious to all possibilities. Intent is a key factor in expectancy, vs. a goal, which is expectation. An intention is an open-ended desire without limits. Intention opens you up to limitless possibilities and outcomes. When you set an intent, your energy is not in "how" it will happen; it's an all-encompassing desire that remains open. It's all-inclusive, and many times it meets not just your desires, but you connect with others where there's a match. When you're in expectancy, you start to see synchronicity in your life. The more you recognize the synchronicity in your life, the more you see it. This is the place were magic really does happen.

In the movie *The Lord of the Rings: The Fellowship of the Ring*,[35] the expectancy is to return Lord Sauron's ring to where it was forged, the fires of Mordor. A team of nine embark on this quest, with Frodo Baggins as the ring bearer. This ring contains concentrated darkness that has power over all who come into contact with it, with the exception of Frodo. His open heart and his goodness protect him from the dark power of this ring and draw others to support him. They see his goodness and trust him. If they fail, the Dark Lord will return to power and take over Middle Earth. Frodo and his team's intent is to return the ring; however, no one knows for sure what will happen to them along the way. It's not clear if they'll make it, or when they'll achieve their intent, but they keep on the journey nonetheless. They stay in expectancy without wavering. It's pointless for them to set a hard schedule for when this will be accomplished. The only time pressure is to get to Mordor as quickly as possible while staying alive. Along the way, each uses his unique skill to help the group continue moving forward. They reach out to others for help and advice, following the steps before them. When they think they're stuck, help comes just in time. Because they're in expectancy, possibilities and solutions present themselves. Regardless of the events that occur, Frodo continues taking the next steps on the journey. At times, he wishes he didn't have this burden, but he never gives up.

In our lives, our opportunity is to set intentions that create sparks of boundless possibilities. At times, we all use goals, thinking they will get us moving and ignite action. Goals can be limited in vision, especially when there's a time limit. Time constraints distract us from accomplishing what we desire, and many times this keeps us from embarking on our journeys in the first place. We want to know the "how," the "when," and the "who" first before we decide if it's a worthy venture or not. Frodo and his team don't lament their time or money constraints; the focus is only on their intent. When they have an opportunity to rest, they rest. They take the time to rejuvenate and also to grieve the loss of their friends.

Friction can ignite a spark that serves and creates magic. Be cautious using time and money as your motivating friction. Many times, using these as the criteria creates such pressure that it overwhelms us and limits our possibilities.

Hugh Jackman is an easy example of how expectancy can play out in one's life. When a producer told him that *The Boy from Oz* musical was returning to Broadway, he got a spark and knew it. He said, "I'm in... I'm doing it. I just knew in my bones when I saw it, this is a great part, I can do this... this is going to be fantastic."[36] Hugh stayed in this expectancy all the way through the production. He didn't listen to the critics or other expert opinions regarding his choice. He continued to follow his spark, and he knew it was for the right reason. Hugh didn't allow time pressures and other career considerations to get in his way. "I feel like we're fully connecting with the audience... people are loving it. I still feel like we're doing it for the right reason."[37] His expectancy was wide open. He didn't go into it with the expectation that he was going to win a Tony. He just knew it was the right part for him. When we make decisions purely on time schedules or financial priorities, we squelch the magic of expectancy. "When something fails and you did it for the wrong reason... [it's] very difficult to live with," says Jackman.[38] The decision to do *The Boy from Oz* was a defining moment in his career. "Everything after that moment was different."[39]

When you're in expectancy, it doesn't mean that you won't experience fear, anger, or other emotions, but being in expectancy helps you move through the emotional cycle more quickly. Think about how this applies on the Emotional Circle of Life diagram from Chapter 3. The outer emotions give you an opportunity to come from a place of response vs. reaction.

Expectancy vs. Expectation

Expectancy is a type of subtle power, the type that attracts that which you desire. *Expectation,* on the other hand, is a make-it-happen-at-all-cost type of power, which is a form of force. Many of us believe that power and force are synonymous. There's a distinct advantage to understanding the differences and employing subtle power in all your life activities.

Think of how you feel when someone tries to coerce you into buying something. Don't you immediately feel some resistance? Compare this to a time when you felt as if you made a connection with a person; they listened to your needs, and you were actually drawn to make the purchase. There's little resistance from this approach. In the first case, the person is trying to make their goal regardless of your wishes. In the second approach, they're inclusive and genuinely desire a win–win outcome. This is a major distinction.

EXPECTANCY	EXPECTATION
Powerful	Forceful
Optimistic	Demanding
Leading	Pressure
Intentional	Calculating
Allowing	Controlling
All Possibilities	Limited Outcome
Flow	Deadline
Valuing	Underrate
Respectful	Incivility
Tolerant	Perfectionist
Anticipate	Worrying
Curious	Certain

Expectancy, like power, is inclusive, whereas expectation is limited to only one outcome.

Staying with this example, here are some behavioral distinctions that show what we mean. The first behavior is probably stuck in the expectation that "I have to meet my goal or else I may lose my job," or "I won't make my bonus," or "I'll look weak among my peers." It's fearful and filled with doubt and anxiety. The second approach comes from a knowing that "people are drawn to me, I always make my goals, and somehow everything always works out for me." This is a confident and powerful way to be. Can you see how one approach is more attractive than the other? Expectancy attracts, and expectation limits. Additionally, one approach is much easier to live with and requires less energy than the other.

Here is a comparison of behaviors to help you recognize when you're in expectancy vs. expectation. We suggest you refer back to this list when you need clarity.

Expectation Meets Expectancy in the Movie Bottle Shock[40]

Bottle Shock is based on the true story of Chateau Montelena during the early days of winemaking in California. Jim Barrett's intent is to make a world-class wine, and he won't give up until he has achieved his dream. The movie starts with Jim telling his loan officer (who is processing his third loan), "It's not about getting it done – it's about getting it done right; it's about making the best goddamn wine we can." That's expectancy, because he wouldn't be going deeper in debt if he wasn't completely certain that this was the next step to realizing his dream.

Steven Spurrier is a British wine merchant in Paris who establishes a publicity event that he expects will get himself known in Paris. He's not selling any wines, and he hopes this event will turn things around for him. Spurrier decides to establish the "Judgment of Paris," a wine-tasting event that compares California wines to the finest French wines. He fully expects the Californian wines to lose.

As Jim Barrett stays in the anger that his dream isn't realized, it actually makes the journey longer and he doesn't see the opportunities in front of him. He switches from anger to the fear that he might fail. He's not happy and is stuck in a groove. His old expectations get in the way and slow him down. Jim is fortunate that his son Bo is able to recognize the opportunities when he can't see them. If Bo hadn't been there to step in and seize the opportunities, Jim's dream would have been delayed. No matter what happens, Bo isn't willing to give up. Through this film, we are reminded how much we need each other, how much we need a community around us, especially when we desire to realize big dreams. No great accomplishment is ever an entirely solo act.

Jim Barrett describes the key to a successful grape: "You want to limit the irrigation because it makes the vines struggle and intensifies the flavor. A comfortable grape, a well-watered fertilized grape, grows into a lazy ingredient of a lousy wine." Jim's wisdom about growing grapes is similar to what's required for a fulfilling life. While the journey can seem challenging, the process is perfect.

We get to see many examples of synchronicity throughout the film. On his own, Jim Barrett couldn't have dreamed up the outcome that positioned his wine in a competition with the finest wines in France. Nor could he have created this event. It came to him in the most unexpected way. Money comes his way just when he needs it.

How Do You Stay In Expectancy and Achieve Your Goals?

By now you may be thinking, "Oh great, so now I stay in expectancy and I'll never get anything done – you've got to be kidding!" The simple answer is: Be clear on your intent, stay open to all possibilities, and be curious. Life changes come at us so quickly sometimes that we get disoriented and forget we've fallen back into expectation. When you recognize that the traits of expectation have returned, remember that you're already moving in the right direction.

Now what do you do? Start focusing on the wins in your life, big or small. Failures are just stepping-stones.

In the movie *Julie & Julia,*[41] we see examples of how to stay in expectancy. In the beginning of the movie, Julie Powell is rattled because all her friends are succeeding and she feels like a failure. She has an unpublished book and hasn't figured out how to make a living with it. While she's discussing her feelings with her husband, she makes amazing meals that both of them enjoy. When her husband suggests that she write about food, Julie shows us how to be open and curious about this idea. Inspiration hits her quickly, and she decides to write about Julia Childs' cookbook. There was little to no resistance in her decision. She loved to cook, she didn't second-guess herself, and she stayed open. She plays with the idea, and we get to enjoy watching her process. Julie decides to cook every recipe in Julia Child's book, and then the objections come: she doesn't eat eggs, she'd have to establish a deadline, it's crazy, etc. Julie's husband doesn't let her go there and continues to encourage her. She wants a deadline, and he tries to convince her not to hang out there. She thinks this deadline is necessary to motivate her to complete the project. We see later in the movie that the deadline doesn't provide the type of motivation she thought it would. She sets an expectation that becomes the driving force, not the process of enjoying the journey. As Julie blogs about herself: "...risking her marriage, her job, and her cat's well-being, she has signed on for a deranged assignment." Julie starts to have meltdowns; the time pressure is starting to get to her. The project is no longer fun – it's stressful and feels like work.

Julia Childs doesn't have to motivate herself to do anything. She loves life, cooking, and people – she is a walking inspiration. As her husband, Paul, says, "Julia brings out the best in a polecat." Julia wants to find something to do with her life, so she tries new things, from hat making and French lessons to playing bridge. She stays open and curious, looking for any spark of inspiration. Julia delightfully enjoys life, and others want to be around her. Julia finds her inspiration by going to cooking school; she writes, "I'm in my third week at the Cordon Bleu and I'm in utter bliss!" Julia discovers that she's fearless and didn't even know it.

We observe the contrast between Julie and Julia. Where Julie's project looks dreadful and hard, Julia's inspires us to want to cook. Julie's deadline leads her to numerous meltdowns. Julia Childs moves through change with ease. She decides to cowrite a cookbook with two friends and finds delight in the process. Julia and Paul must move from Paris to Marseilles to Germany, and she writes: "There's no chance that we'll meet our deadline – it will be at least two more years." She makes no excuses, and it doesn't seem to bother her. Julia continues to enjoy her life as she and Paul are relocated around Europe. Even when her publisher doesn't like the revised book, Julia says, "Oh, well, boo-hoo, now what?" She moves on effortlessly to her next adventure, becoming a television chef.

Julie Powell becomes completely depressed when she hears a reporter allege that Julia Childs hates her blog. Prior to receiving this call, she had over sixty calls asking to publish her book. But it was this one call that upset her and stole her happiness. Who knows if Ms. Childs even said she hated it – that was irrelevant to Julie.

Julie Powell gives us a clear example of how we set goals and expectations, thinking they'll get us the progress we desire. Setting goals is taught as the formula of making it happen and realizing success. She establishes a deadline, believing it will insure completion of her project. Now, you might be thinking that she was successful and got what she wanted, right? Yes, it's possible to achieve your goals this way, but it's heavier, it takes more energy, and it requires constant focus to keep yourself motivated.

Instead, Julia Childs was always looking for the joy in a situation, and if there wasn't any, she chose something different. Ms. Child's journey looks effortless compared to Julie Powell's, and she definitely was having more fun. When it was time for Julia to move on to something else, the doors opened for her and she was in the right place at the right time. She was open to all possibilities and her curiosity continued to introduce her to a new adventures. She also found herself surrounded by people that enjoyed her company and loved life too.

Most of us can relate to Julie Powell; we try to make our lives work out similarly. We set rigid expectations, thinking this will keep us moving towards the goals we desire to achieve. Perhaps this why many of us are inspired by people like Julia Childs. We can't understand how they stay so joyful and how life seems effortless and always works out for them. The truth is, we all have obstacles or sorrows, but it's a matter of focus. Julia wanted children, but for whatever reason, that didn't happen. Her focus is on enjoying life, not on the parts of her life that didn't go as desired. That's why she can move on from one change to the next.

Motivation and Inspiration

In the chart below, we describe the process of motivation and inspiration. As you can see, ease of lift is the lightness that comes from being inspired. You feel called to something and if you're present, it can lead you to a new way. Motivation is how you get yourself to take the next right action. When you're deep in a groove of expectation, it's as if the only way out is to take the next step in front of you – and that's where motivation comes in. Expectation takes more effort and can be a longer process than expectancy. It can seem like climbing out of a hole and up the mountain of progress. Each step takes you closer to being above ground, where eventually you'll get back to light and being centered. Once you're above ground, you have opportunities for inspiration, opportunities to get the wind at your back and soar. While you can still use motivation to keep pushing up the mountain, staying in expectancy opens you up for gusts of inspiration which can take you up the mountain of progress with less effort and more quickly

INSPIRATION
Ease of Lift

Joy
Julia Childs
Light

EASE OF EXPECTANTCY

Steps of Expectation
Julie Powell

PROGRESS

MOTIVATION
Effort & Challenge — Heavy

Be Open to Receive

Creating your dreams and goals from a place of expectancy is a powerful way to live life. A critical component to this process is being open to receive from wherever or whoever may want to give. So many of us get stopped in our tracks with this concept. We may feel it's morally better to give than receive. Some of us just don't feel worthy to receive. Others have such limiting attitudes that they deflect any goodness that might come their way. At times, we all probably fit into these categories, depending on where we are at any given moment.

Being receptive to receiving is a big topic with many facets. We recommend starting in the area of attitude. Some of us have a life practice of looking for the downside to anything happening to us. Perhaps we received this pattern from our family members. Sometimes it seems like the intellectually rational way to see life. Many of us are simply not aware that we're "half-glass empty" type of people. Regardless of where you learned this habit, it blocks the goodness that's all around you and limits your ability to receive.

In the movie *On Golden Pond,*[42] Norman Thayer, Jr. (Henry Fonda) plays a retired professor in a long-term marriage to Ethel Thayer (Katherine Hepburn). Norman is a virtuoso curmudgeon and has clearly refined this way of being into an art form. His biting sarcasm always ends with clever wit. A small dose of his demeanor can be funny, but he doles out a constant stream of it. He's also afraid of dying. As Ethel tells Norman, "You've been talking about death ever since we met."

Norman and Ethel have a vacation home on Golden Pond. They've been coming here for over forty years. As they return for the spring, Ethel enthusiastically asks Norman if he can hear the loons welcoming them back. He responds, "I don't hear a thing." Norman would rather stay inside reading his paper then join his wife at the lake. He's not having any fun with life, and his attitude is not attractive.

Ethel is light and airy. She loves life, and Norman's crankiness doesn't seem to ever affect her. She calls him her "Ole Poop" and goes on blissfully about her day. Other times she calls him her "knight in shinning armor." Ethel sees and hears nature's beauty, finds berries in the woods, and can be caught singing and dancing for no apparent reason. Ethel's attitude is positive, and she has retained a childlike view on life. It still amazes her and she loves being alive. She's a joy to be around, and others benefit from her good humor. This is what staying in expectancy looks like.

It's Norman's eightieth birthday, and their middle-aged daughter Chelsea (Jane Fonda) is returning to their summer home to celebrate. Chelsea believes that Norman wished she had been a boy. She laments the lack of connection she has with him and gets stuck in this groove. As a result, she stays away for long periods of time. Chelsea is unwilling to change her attitude or thinking about Norman and the childhood she didn't get. He didn't live up to her expectation of a good dad.

Chelsea begins to change her viewpoint when her mother gives her some wise advice. She says, "Chelsea, you have a great big chip on your shoulder which is very unattractive.... You stay away for years at a time and never come home... and when you do all you can do is be disagreeable about the past."

Ethel asks, "What's the point?" Her wise advice gets through to Chelsea. "Everyone looks back on their childhood with a certain amount of bitterness and... it doesn't have to ruin your life, darling." She says, "You're a big girl now – aren't you tired of it all? Life marches by, Chels... I suggest you get on with it."

Chelsea is more like her father than she recognizes. While he was cranky, fearing death, she was stuck in the past, lamenting what could have been. Both attitudes are examples of how we block the goodness that life has to offer. We want to realize our dreams, but we can't see how our attitudes are big barriers – fences so high that abundance is prevented from coming to us. We're not available in the moment and thus miss the opportunities that are all around us.

Chelsea comes around and begins to accept Norman as he is. This opens up exchanges of love with her father that she didn't expect.

When Norman's heart gives him a scare, he begins to realize how lucky he is to be with such a delightful companion. A willingness to enjoy life starts to seep in. We see how this is a wakeup call to Norman, as he says, "Ethel, listen, the loons, they've come around to say good-bye."

On Golden Pond is a beautiful movie with many messages. It's not a surprise that it won so many awards in 1981. If you haven't seen this movie in a while, you may enjoy seeing it again from the perspective we've discussed. ▨

❈ CHAPTER SUMMARY ❈

In this chapter, there are many examples that show how the process is perfect in the long run. Even so, you may still be thinking, "How can it be perfect when an event (job loss, divorce, house repossession, or illness) has totally ruined my life? I'm miserable – how can that be perfect?" This may be feather-like guidance, or it may be a two-by-four that's trying to perfectly stir you to your own unique process. We'll go into this concept in our next chapter.

BELIEF STATEMENTS REPRESENTED IN THIS CHAPTER:

Energizing Beliefs

❖ I am allowed to reevaluate my life and take the time to discern my feelings when moments of clarity present themselves.

❖ I love living my life openly and honestly.

❖ People just want me to be myself, and the rest of the stuff doesn't matter.

❖ When I'm asked to begin a new journey, I don't hesitate and go immediately.

❖ I know I always have a choice, and I let go of others' opinions to the contrary.

❖ There is much I don't understand, so I trust my inner knowing and take the actions that inspire me.

❖ I stay present in the moment, and I'm always ready for whatever happens.

❖ I celebrate when the moments present themselves, and I don't let the challenges of my life get in the way of these moments.

❖ I am at peace and know that I did the best I could.

❖ I focus on the delightful future I'm creating.

❖ I stay open and curious about all my ideas.

❖ I help my teammates by considered and thoughtful action.

De-Energizing Beliefs

❖ If I can make my life look perfect on the outside, others won't know how miserable I am inside.

❖ If I lost everything, my life would be over.

❖ Diverse cultures, beliefs, and sexual preferences threaten me.

❖ People that think for themselves are dangerous.

❖ I feel stuck in my marriage and don't know how to get out.

❖ If I spread my wings like a butterfly, I'm afraid I'll draw too much attention and will be crushed by the world.

❖ I feel like I'm in a slow death since my life changed, and I'm afraid it will always be this way.

❖ There's no outlet for my grief.

❖ I feel really alone most of the time.

❖ People don't want to know how I really feel and can't handle the truth.

❖ I allow my old expectations to get in my way and slow me down.

❖ I second-guess my new adventure.

❖ I only want things to go my way.

❖ I push the pain away so hard that I disconnect myself from the ones I love.

❖ I'm just an old grouch, and that's all I'll ever be.

❖ I'll receive when I know who, what, where, when, and how.

❖ I say mean things to keep others from getting too close to me.

❖ I put on a tough exterior to keep others intimidated.

❖ I can't have fun and play because it might turn into some form of competition.

❖ I'm impatient and yell at others when things don't go my way.

❖ Why didn't my childhood work out perfectly?

MUSIC SELECTION

"Spring Again," Lanae Hale

"Golden Slumbers," sung by k.d. lang

"Yesterday," the Beatles

"Autrefois," Pink Martini

"Gloria (1st movement)" sung by The City of London Singers with John Rutter

ESSENTIAL OIL RECOMMENDATION

Eucalyptus radiata: Cooling, refreshing, and energizing.

Rosemary: University of Miami scientists found that inhaling rosemary boosted alertness, eased anxiety, and amplified analytic and mental ability.

Believe: Helps to release the unlimited potential everyone possesses, making it possible to more fully experience health, happiness, and vitality.

Grounding: Creates a feeling of solidity and balance. It stabilizes and grounds us in order to cope constructively with reality.

Sacred Mountain: Instills strength, empowerment, grounding, and protection with a calming connection to nature.

CHAPTER 5

The Feather or the Two-by-Four: You Choose

"The fates lead him who will; him who won't, they drag."
— Seneca "

An emotional breakdown is a highly underrated spiritual experience" — Marianne Williamson

Do life changes seem to come out of nowhere and catch you off guard? They might seem so big that you feel like you just took a blow by a two-by-four. In our experience, however, we've found that major changes don't usually come out of nowhere; typically there was gentle guidance along the way that was missed. We call this guidance *feathers* and the not-so-gentle traumatic events *two-by-fours*.

Feathers are our guidance. They start out as gentle awarenesses, discernments, hints, suggestions from others, etc. If we don't catch these feathers that are trying to guide us to gently change our trajectory, we eventually encounter two-by-four events that continue until we make a change, willingly or not. Ideally, if we get better at recognizing the feather-like guidance that is all around us, we move through it, grow, and change with less resistance. Remember, life is seasonal and change is inevitable. The more skilled you can become at recognizing these normal changes in life, the quicker you can get back to joy.

The benefit of looking for the feathers is that this provides maximum control in your life. The more you're not aware of or don't pay attention to the feathers, the more you can't see the solutions to any outcome. This becomes analogous to getting hit by a truck, being picked up in an ambulance, and taken to the hospital. At this point, you are no longer in control of the situation. You are experiencing a two-by-four event.

There are many ways we miss the feathers, but they are all based in our beliefs and values. Your beliefs can be a house of cards because you fight for them. We defend our beliefs as if they are an absolute set of rules and then, ironically, only act on them only if it suits our purpose.

Feathers come in many shapes and sizes. Think of these feathers as the contrast that helps us see when something isn't right. We all have our own unique feathers, but the following is a list that we've found are common in our human experience.

The Feather of Body Pain

When your body is hurting in any area, it's a feather telling you to take a look at what is going on – regardless of the degree of pain. An increase in frequency is a feather getting more insistent. If you don't listen, it just gets bigger and will lead to more problems and upsets. Pain is a feather from your body that there's something that needs attention, so don't delay and get it checked out.

For example, Sue-Anne once had a client who was having chest pain. She had it checked out, and medically she was fine. Her client came to recognize that her chest hurt whenever she was fighting herself about something. This became her way of knowing that she was getting some guidance, and then she would take action by working with Sue-Anne.

The Feather of Exhaustion

This feather occurs because we're condensing too much into one day (or a series of days) without enough rest. This is becoming a required skill for the successful modern person. We try to leverage every minute of the day, and we see this as a strength. When we become exhausted, our emotions tend to be more reactive and erratic. For men, this typically looks like anger, whereas for women, it can result in unexplained tears. If you notice that your emotions seem erratic, it may be the feather of exhaustion trying to get your attention. Many times, we try to manage this feather with caffeine, power drinks, adrenaline, nicotine, and sheer will-power. If you find yourself needing any of these tools on a consistent basis, this is a feather telling you to create some rest or unscheduled time with yourself or others.

The Feather of Judgment

This feather lets you know that it's time to take a look at your beliefs. The best way to maintain peace of mind and body is to stay out of judgment of self and others. Judgment is similar to a parasite — you don't know you have it and you're not aware of how it is draining your energy. Like a parasite, once you're aware of it, you take steps to eradicate it and immediately feel better with more energy.

Judgment is one way we try to control others' behavior, and there is no peace or freedom in it. We want them not to behave a certain way so we can feel better — which does not work, because we must be able to feel better regardless of what others do. Otherwise, we end up having less freedom, because we've lost a sense of where we are on the emotional scale. When you are judging positively or negatively about anything, you limit where you can go with your emotional state. Now you have to judge something as good or bad to determine where you allow yourself to go emotionally. If you judge someone as good, you have to access the feeling of joy whether you feel it or not. This now means that you try to control every action that is happening around you so you can attempt to keep yourself happy and joyful.

If it's behavior you judge as wrong, perhaps the other person will feel shame and then you can influence their behavior so you can feel good again. Either way, you relinquish your emotional power to someone else, resulting in less freedom. See your judgments as imposing your own personal value system — which you measure everything by — on others.

In the movie *RV*,[43] we see an example of how one family judges another. The family being judged, the Gornickes (Mary Jo, Travis, Earl, Moon, and Billy) do not buy into the judgment of the other family. In fact, Mary Jo Gornicke (Kristin Chenoweth) was able to constantly find something redeeming. Eventually, the Munro family (Bob, Jamie, Cassie, and Carl) was able to see that the Gornickes were much happier than they were.

RV shows us that love always prevails – it is the only thing that wins. You cannot achieve change by pulling yourself down to the level of negativity. Sometimes we forget that our true nature is love and that judgment takes energy to resist this love. You block off your inner goodness, and this takes energetic effort to resist. When we don't allow this honest flow through our energetic system, it cannot flow easily and it takes effort because we have to pinch it off in different places to hold that judgment. It takes energy to hold that resistance against whatever you are feeling or whatever someone is doing, and we're not aware of it.

If you simply flowed from a place of allowing that total love to be exuded, you'd spend less time in judgment. This does not mean you are in the clouds and ungrounded; it does not mean you will not have discernment. You will still choose what you will play or not play with, but you don't judge it. When we can move from judgment to discernment, then we are moving from reactivity to response. Discernment is the quality of being able to grasp and comprehend what is obscure. It's the power to see what is not evident in an everyday mind. It's obscure because you bypass your value systems of right and wrong. This means that you make conscious choices vs. reactive unconscious choices.

In This Time of Reason, We Think Truth Lies in Judgment

Society has created a set of interrelated values, and we tend to measure everything that happens against it. Our values have become rigid over time, until now they are simply a set of beliefs. There have been times in history when people had a better understanding of how things flow because of their connection to nature. As a result, they naturally accepted how energy works. In our modern time, we have shut that down because we think everything should be filtered through the mind. We would be better served if we stopped and considered what our soul thinks or what our body feels.

If you can't recognize your own judgments, let's start with an easy one. Sex scandals of the rich and famous are examples of our judgments on autopilot. We feel like celebrities should live up to a standard that's above what we expect from ourselves. Because they are powerful, we think they should be better than us. We see them as godlike, with superhuman powers. When they don't live up to this standard, we judge that they shouldn't get to enjoy fame and fortune anymore.

We continue to perpetuate this by reacting to media outbursts as if this is important. If we just ignored this type of news, we'd see less of it. But why don't we ignore it? Maybe we secretly enjoy seeing them fail. As Lady Gaga told Anderson Cooper on *60 Minutes*, "Everybody wants to see the decay of the superstar... they want to see me fail, they want to see me fall on stage.... Isn't that the age that we live in? ...We want to see people who have it all lose it all."[44]

In the Australian culture, this is known as the "tall poppy syndrome." They've exceeded us at this level, we're jealous, and then we want to chop them down in size. Maybe we just don't see their humanity any longer and have forgotten that they have the same needs and desires as we do.

How Should Someone Respond to Hurtful, Harmful, Unpleasant Behavior?

Always look for something redeeming in the person. This does not mean condoning the behavior, but you do not judge it. We all accept the adage "What goes around comes around." The place of no-judgment helps us all discover compassion within. It helps us see that we're all on different paths, learning lessons at various stages.

REACTIVITY TO RESPONSE IN ACTION
VICTIM/PERPETRATOR

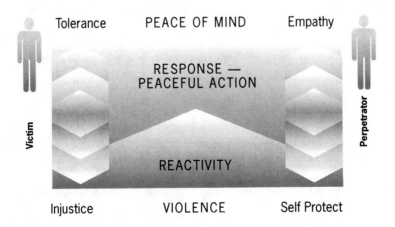

Victim vs. Perpetrator — What Role Are You Playing?

Victim and perpetrator are opposing roles that complete the whole and allow us to learn. In the US, the civil rights movement helped African-Americans to come to a place of strength and peaceful resistance, which was the balancing point of power. This balanced victim feelings within the people and kept them from choosing violence. Dr. King, James Farmer, Jr., and others continued to lead the people in this balance. Instead of being perpetrators, they taught empathy and understanding, while at the same time utilizing and improving the laws. Once you start fighting against injustice, you slide back into the victim role and play the dance all over again. Somehow, these leaders seemed to understand the power of this balance. As Byron Katie says, victims are violent people and "defense is the first act of war."[45] The balance between victim and perpetrator is peace of mind, and this allows us to respond rather than react.

Looking at the chart, if you're in the victim role, tolerance will be your path to peace of mind. If you happen to be playing to perpetrator role, empathy will move you from reactivity to thoughtful response. We all take turns in these roles. The more we can recognize them, the quicker we can respond in ways that serve us and others better.

The Feather of Bondage

You can be in bondage to other people's judgments or to your own. Have you made something in your external life the master other than yourself? Do you feel that you're not free and there's nothing you can do about it? Do you feel like you've made some life decisions that now mean you can't choose again? If you answered yes to any of these questions, this is a feather trying to guide you. Sometimes you fall into bondage and don't even realize it. All you know is that you don't feel free. Our work life is an easy place to see this play out. We think we have to conform to the company culture and do as they say, even if this means going against our desires. If we don't, we're afraid we'll lose our job or be stuck in the same job for the remainder of our career. Many times we feel the feather of bondage in our relationships or marriages.

Usually bondage symptoms register like fear. We're afraid to even consider a different choice and thus feel imprisoned. This happens because we're all trying to conform to whatever traditions we're a part of: society, family, religion, company, etc. We then measure everything we desire against the norms of our tradition. As a result, we don't see that there are other options for our life. This can become a groove in itself that distorts reality for us.

In the movie *Get Low*,[46] Felix Bush (Robert Duvall) lives the life of a hermit for forty years. He doesn't have any family or friends. Felix lives in a log cabin in the mountains, and his only contact is his mule Gracie. One evening, Felix believes that he's dying and decides to spend his last night with his beloved mule. When he awakens in the morning, Felix decides he wants freedom before he passes. His solution is to throw his own funeral party. He wants to hear what others have to say about him while he is still alive. He also hopes to tell the secret that changed the course of his life. He reaches out to his preacher friend, Reverend Charlie Jackson, and asks him to speak for him in case he's unable to tell the story himself. When his friend refuses, Felix doesn't want to go through with the party. Reverend Jackson doesn't want to be a part of the funeral because Felix has not asked for forgiveness in the prescribed way. Both men display an affection and bond for each other, yet this secret has kept them apart for forty years.

Felix hires the town funeral director, Frank Quinn (Bill Murray) and his partner, Buddy, to coordinate all the details of this party. Buddy finds Felix's story curious and wants to discover why any man would cut himself off from society in such an extreme way. In one scene, Buddy asks Felix, "What are you doing?" and Felix replies, "Going through the motions... there's alive and there's dead, and there's a worse place in between." Felix has been going through the motions for forty years. He was so ashamed of his actions that he exiled himself.

Often we take our traditions literally and believe that we must adhere to their rules to live an acceptable life. As Reverend Jackson says, "We like to imagine that good and bad, right and wrong, are miles apart. But the truth is, very often they are all tangled up with each other." We don't realize that the rules of a tradition are less important than its intended purpose. Our traditions serve as a compass to provide guidance along the way. When we see them as rigid rules, we lose all freedom to see our situation from another perspective. We won't allow any compassion for ourselves because we broke the rules. As a result, our choices can become limited or, as in Felix's case, lead to a life without human contact and love.

If you recognize the feather of bondage in your life, take a look at your priorities and get clear on what is most important. Check in with your emotions and notice how you feel about any area where you feel imprisoned. Recognize the fact that, no matter the situation, you always have other choices. Embrace this truth and feel how freeing it is, and then start looking for options.

The Feather of Self-Judgment

Self-judgment is a way of beating yourself up. Do you ever achieve anything when you beat yourself up? You definitely feel worse about the situation, and then you start heading down the negative side of the number line. You slip down the scale, thinking that feeling bad will motivate you. In other words, you are trying to intimidate yourself. It's as if you are trying to be the authoritarian father or mother, intimidating yourself until you eventually coerce yourself into doing the "right" thing. But you are actually just creating another form of resistance within yourself. This approach doesn't work.

There is new research suggesting that self-compassion improves our health and well-being. "I found in my research that the biggest reason people aren't more self-compassionate is that they are afraid they'll become self-indulgent," said Dr. Kristen Neff, an associate professor of human development at the University of Texas at Austin. "They believe that self-criticism is what keeps them in line. Most people have gotten it wrong, because our culture says being hard on yourself is the way to be."[47]

Think of putting pressure on a jack-in-the-box. As the pressure continues to push, the lid eventually pops off. We trick ourselves into believing that if we push ourselves down long enough, maybe we'll come through to the other side, learn the lesson we desired, and then have peace. There are those who have taken this path, but we assure you that it takes longer. The path is excruciatingly difficult and it's easy to get stuck in rage. If you've read Byron Katie's work or Eckhart Tolle's, they both describe similar scenarios.

Judging yourself from a place of guilt, anger, resentment, and remorse doesn't necessarily motivate you to do good. These emotions actually motivate you to react. As a result, your self-judgment blocks your ability to respond.

We have this idea in our western culture that if someone feels guilty about what they did, they won't do it again. But that is not the truth. Instead, if you feel guilty about what you did, that's the energy you put out, and you just attract more of the same. There is nothing wrong with saying to yourself, "Wow, that was a poor choice; I want to try that again and choose differently the next time." That has a different energy than regret or guilt – it separates the facts about what happened from your response/reaction to those facts.

When you can look at what happened (or what you did, or what somebody did to you) and place no value judgment on it, then you can discern the facts. As Columbo always said, "Just the facts, ma'am, just the facts." Think of two children hitting each other. One comes and says, "Well, he hit me first." The other one says, "Yes, but you started it by making a face at me." And so it goes back and forth. The facts are simply that one child hit the other child, and one child made a face at the other child. With this approach you are able to say, "All right, none of it is working. Your behavior isn't working, and yours isn't working either. What would you like to do differently?" But if you get into a value system of "You should not have made a face" and "You should not be hitting," all you have done is slip into judgment. Neither child has been heard because you have invoked your own value system of how someone should not behave in a certain way. When you are in any form of judgment, you have just removed any opportunity for freedom, because you are trying to control the behavior.

You know you're judging yourself when you get an emotional charge from your own self-talk. You're trying to control your own behavior by being hypercritical. You can't judge yourself into self-acceptance – you can't judge yourself into a place of feeling good. Regrets are another form of self-judgment. They are effectively a waste of time because the past is crippling you in the present.

The Feather of Others' Opinions

This feather shows up when you are concerned about others' opinions because you're scared they will judge you. You're effectively putting their opinions above your own discernment. Everyone is allowed opinions, but you have a choice to discern the benefit for yourself and not react to what isn't right for you. When people offer opinions, they really do believe they're helping. Many times, this is the way they show their love for you the best way they can – they mean well. This is not to say that you shouldn't welcome advice; we all learn from those around us. The key is to make a distinction between advice and opinions. The former can be the source of learning, whereas the latter can distort your own discernment.

The Feather of Pleasing

If you're hypersensitive to what other people think, you probably react by trying to please. Trying to please others can feel like a dog chasing its tail – you're just going around in circles. If you recognize this feather, simply stop trying to please others. Follow your own inner guidance and deal with your anxiety when you fear others won't approve. Remember, when you're trying to please others, you've negated your own internal guidance system. You've put your compass in other people's hands, hoping it will all work out. Unfortunately, you'll never be able to please anyone but yourself, so just stop trying and tap into your own guidance. This is the place where you'll discover lasting joy.

The Feather of Vanity

Vanity is defined as excessive pride in or admiration of one's appearance or achievements. Often you get the guidance of this feather but can't see it. You know this feather is present when you find yourself defending your image, identity, job, etc. Vanity opens you up to being manipulated; it fogs your discernment and limits your instincts. Remember, when you're fearful about anything, others can get to you in subtle ways. Vanity is the by-product of insecurity and fear. When you're not secure in yourself, you become reactive to what people say about you (whether it's good or bad).

"I Don't Pick It Up, I Don't Lay It Down"

As Dr. Maya Angelou told David Chappelle:

"One of the things I've learned, or am even still in the process of learning, is 'don't pick it up and don't lay it down.' When someone says, 'You're the best, you're the greatest, you're the most wonderful, you're the finest artist of the time, blah, blah, blah, you say 'Ah.' If you pick that up, you also have to pick it up when they say, 'You're nothing, you've lost it, you used to be it, what happened?' So I don't pick it up, I don't lay it down."[8]

Vanity gives meaning to the opinions you receive. Everyone has a right to his or her opinions. Your job is to become a bystander, an observer. If you feel good or bad about yourself because of what someone thinks of you, there may be some vanity involved. There aren't enough people's opinions in the world that can truly make you feel good or bad. There's nothing wrong with being lifted up or inspired by others. Inspiration is a choice you make that fills you up, and it is usually unrelated to what someone has said about you. Vanity is an unconscious, bottomless cup, and many times it just brings on more reactivity. When you recognize this feather, step back and detach yourself from what others say about you, regardless whether it's criticism or accolades.

The Feather of Doubt

Doubt causes you to go back into the past or try to judge the future you are projecting. Doubting yourself keeps you stuck and unable to be open to all possibilities. Realize that this is simply an indicator that something requires your attention.

Doubt cramps energy. Think about what happens when you step on a hose of running water. The water can no longer flow. Our bodies are like the hose – the water is the emotional energy in our system. Doubt is the equivalent of pinching off your energetic hose. You become rigid and closed off. Over time, your doubts can also become a new unconscious truth that you live by. This type of thinking keeps you stuck in your groove and limits your choices.

The Feather of Blame

Blame is a result of not allowing yourself to admit that you made a mistake. In the times we live in, we're discouraged for acknowledging error because it may end up in litigation, thus limiting options for defense. There's no credibility in admitting you made a mistake; you're not allowed to. So we all end up playing the musical blame game, going around and around.

The Feather of Guilt

Self-imposed stereotypes are the source of beliefs. The same belief can generate different emotions, depending on its stereotype reference. Your family's belief system is your primary belief container. Religion, money, status, job, race, nationality, etc., all fit under family belief systems. If you're aligned with your family system, you feel innocent. When you're not aligned with your family system, you feel guilty.

Guilt, like all of our emotions, is different for each one of us, because it's related to how we were raised in our unique family system. Guilt is the result of breaking the family norms in behavior and emotions. Until you make peace with these, you'll still feel guilt and self-judgment.

The Feather of Duty

The feather of duty often trumps truth and honoring one's word. Throughout history, wars have been started, religions defended, and family members killed – all in the name of duty. Duty is defined as a moral or legal obligation. Duty has become an honorable thing to fight for at all costs, regardless how it affects your country, your family, or your life. We can all fall into this trap in our jobs, politics, cultural beliefs, and religious practices.

When we defend our duty, the actions that follow are usually reactive and unconscious. Yet somehow, since it stems from a place of duty, the ends justify the means. Duty always means well, but it usually clouds the truth and opens us up to manipulation. Who doesn't want to be seen as a righteous and honorable person who fights for what is right? We create monuments and legends for individuals that have taken this path. Duty can be a one-dimensional solution that limits outcomes that might serve everyone in a better way. When we hold strongly to our own sense of duty, how do we find common ground with someone who has an opposing yet equally strong sense of righteous duty? How do you see from a new perspective when duty gets intensified? When duty goes head-to-head, everyone loses and no one wins.

The movie *Fair Game*[49] is based on the true story of Ambassador Joseph C. Wilson (Sean Penn) and Valerie Plame (Naomi Watts) and what transpires when Mr. Wilson writes an op-ed piece in *The New York Times*. Mr. Wilson's piece was written in response to how his field research had been used to justify going to war in Iraq. He felt his information had been misused, and he wanted to set the record straight, even though publicly no one knew for sure that it was his information. Joe Wilson felt a sense of duty to tell the truth about the lack of evidence that led to the war. He personally had been involved in some of the research, and he takes on the White House's explanation of why the US had a duty to go to war.

Clearly, the White House's position was that it had a duty to save and protect our country at all costs. This has been a strong and reinforced position for many administrations. When Joe Wilson meets this level of duty head on, both sides reactively take action to defend their position, bringing chaos to all involved, especially the Wilson family. While all this is going on, other values get trampled too. People's careers are ruined, and institutions begin to react with fear and protection. This makes discerning truth almost impossible. Everyone is reacting, defending their position, and trying to win the battle of truth.

If you find yourself caught up in duty in any area of your life, step back and take a look at your situation from every perspective. Take time to discern what is going on, and don't get reactive. Duty rarely leads to truth; it usually just leads to another exchange of fire.

The Feather of Pressure

As we came together to write our book, it took time to find our flow. We needed to discover a process that allowed both of us to collaborate while honoring each other's individual process. We pooled our financial resources together and embarked on this journey together, not knowing how long it would take.

At first, we didn't establish a time frame of when we desired to complete our book. At the time, we felt the pressure would have been too much and would most likely have kept us from the project altogether. We eventually recognized when it was time to establish a target day for completion. Our book was taking form, we knew our financial resources couldn't sustain the project much longer, and we were ready to be done. We decided to call it a "target" and not a deadline because the former felt more empowering than the latter. Additionally, we both knew that a certain amount of pressure was necessary. Establishing this target date worked; it provided just enough pressure to enable us to complete the manuscript on time. It also freed both of us up in enough time to pursue other sources of income to sustain ourselves while the book went into publication.

The key to the feather of pressure is to recognize that some pressure can be too much. Think of what happens when you are cleaning a wood table. Too much rubbing ruins the finish, and too little doesn't get it clean enough. It's a balance you have to discover. This is how we used the feather of pressure to help us complete this book.

There's another type of pressure that also guides you. It's a type of work or relationship pressure that starts to affect your sleep and your quality of life. When you feel that your life becomes what Sue-Anne calls "work and recover," this is another type of feather of pressure guidance to take seriously.

The Feather of Resisting What Is

You cannot achieve change by matching another individual at their set point on any specific issue. When you go into resistance mode, you are trying to match someone where they are, in their negativity. This negativity takes energy to resist, and it blocks off your goodness.

In the movie *The Josephine Baker Story*,[50] an extraordinarily talented entertainer pushes against the establishment of the times.

The harder she pushes, the more struggle she endures. This doesn't bring her peace and joy – it ultimately isolates her.

There are modern-day examples of leaders that didn't resist the establishment and yet found a powerful way to influence change. Yes, this approach can take longer, but think of the impact the following people have had on history: Gandhi, Nelson Mandela, Dr. Martin Luther King, Jr., Aung San Suu Kyi, and the Dalai Lama. All of these inspirational leaders knew that power came from taking their time and not from forcing change. So many times we want change *now*, but we only have to look at nature as an example to see that formative change takes longer. Trying to force an outcome might achieve a short-term desire, but it's much harder and the cost can be too great.

If you recognize that your mind is spinning and ruminating about a topic over and over again, you're most likely resisting what is. If you're ready to work on this pattern in a deeper way, we recommend Byron Katie's *Loving What Is*[51i] and her process called "The Work." We've both enjoyed her teachings and think you will too.

The Feather of Reactivity

Pay attention to your reactivity, especially if you see it reoccurring over the same situation. This helps you to see that something needs to change about the situation. Follow the reactivity, and you'll learn what's not working within you. Remember, it's not other people's fault that you're being reactive. See your reactivity as a guidepost to patterns you desire to leave behind.

The Feather of Time

Following the ebb and flow of time is similar to sailing. You catch the wind when it's there and wait when it's not. No sailor tries to create or force the wind. When there's no wind, sailors don't jump out and start paddling. If they did, who would enjoy sailing? Flowing with time can be like harnessing the wind. You get better and better at taking action when the wind is there and resting when it's not.

This also helps you to connect with others' timing, which sparks synchronicity. For instance, you're running late for a meeting because of a traffic jam or some other delay. When you arrive at your appointment, it turns out that the meeting is late in starting anyway. If you notice occurrences like this, it means that you're flowing with the feather of time. The more you practice, the better you'll get at harnessing this feather. Remember, it's not about *making* it happen, it's recognizing what's happening and stepping into it with ease.

The Feather of Having to Be Right

You'll recognize this feather when you find yourself being defensive about any issue in your life. This is a sign you might be thinking it's important that you are right and that others realize they're wrong.

The Feather of Pushing Too Much

If you notice that you're pushing uphill, not gaining momentum, and increasingly becoming exhausted in any area of your life, this can be a feather trying to guide you to stop and take a break, look at what's going on, and regroup.

In our western culture, vacations have become an endurance test to be conquered. Since we take so few vacations, we try to jam as much as we can into one experience. What's supposed to be a restful and rejuvenating period can become all about achieving as much sightseeing as possible. The experience of enjoying each moment becomes secondary to the need to maximize the experience. It's not uncommon for us to be exhausted from our vacation experiences. If you can relate to feeling this way, it's possible you're pushing too hard.

Many times we push ourselves because we're like divers trying to find pearls. The pearls can be the job position you desire, it could be a body weight goal, or it even can be attaining spiritual awareness. When you're diving for pearls, remember that if you go too deep and stay underwater too long, it can be very harmful. Pearl divers know they have limited time in certain depths, so they don't stay too long. We encourage you to dive for your pearls in life, but just recognize when you're pushing too deep and take a break.

Miss the Feathers and You Get Cooked

When we miss the feather-like guidance in our lives, some of us enter the next phase, which we call "getting cooked." When you're being cooked emotionally, it seems like everything is falling apart. It appears there's no wiggling out of some situations, as if you're in a pot of water with the temperature rising slowly. This is when you know that growth is upon you. It's the divine formula.

Being cooked is a slow process analogous to the "boiling frog syndrome." In 1872, scientists demonstrated that a normal frog would not attempt to escape if the water was heated slowly enough, and this was corroborated in 1875. This metaphor is used to suggest that if we don't recognize the change that is gradually upon us, we'll suffer undesirable consequences. We call these two-by-four events. In recent studies, however, most frogs recognized that they were being cooked and quickly took action to get out of the pot. Ideally, this is our hope, too – we will recognize that the cooking has begun and choose differently.

What to Do When You Recognize You're Being Cooked?

When it's getting hot, take it easy. We have a perfect example of one thing you can do. When we wrote this book, it was not unusual for the Texas summer temperatures to be around 100 degrees. You know how active squirrels can be, but when it's hot, they find a place to rest, slow down, and cool off. The squirrel provides an example of one thing you can do when you notice you're being cooked. This is not the time for sporadic, unfocused action. Slow down, cool off, and see where it takes you.

Being cooked gives you strength of mind and heart, which enables you to have the ability to respond and take right action instead of react. As the saying goes, whatever doesn't kill you makes you stronger. Looking at everything as serving a purpose is a way of helping you to stay sane. Service can be easy, while staying sane sometimes is not. A doctor lancing a boil is painful, but it does release what is causing the boil.

Avoid beating yourself up for where you have been, and be peaceful and grateful for your new understanding.

Cooking serves us by heightening our awareness of the growth that is upon us. It also helps us begin the eventual melting of the emotions in our bodies. There is a physical aspect to this; just like in cooking, when you heat ice, it turns to water and flows again.

The Art of Recognizing the Release of Frozen Emotions

Think of releasing frozen emotions as bursting bubbles within the body. How do you know you're releasing and bursting emotional bubbles? The emotion is disproportionate to the event at hand. The intensity comes out of the blue and is irrational. We discussed what this look like in Chapter 3 when we looked at the character of Bertie in *The King's Speech*. He's a good example of what this releasing looks like.

Sue-Anne helps her clients recognize when their emotions have started to defrost. It's analogous to a freezer that's built up ice over time. If you try to pick at the ice and force it out, you cause damage to the freezer. The best way to remove the ice is to allow it to thaw and defrost. When your emotions are releasing, it can feel similar to the sensation that one of your legs or arms were "sleeping." That pins-and-needle feeling is your body waking up, and it hurts until it's fully awake. Releasing your emotions can feel like this; it's your body recovering. Engaging the services of a massage therapist and/or chiropractor can help with this process.

We were fortunate that Dr. Tom Lenehan, Sue-Anne's spouse, was able to help us during the writing of this book. We experienced much of the releasing we're describing, and it took a toll on us physically. Dr. Tom's skill as a chiropractor and expertise in working with the energetic releasing of emotions was integral to keeping us going.

The way we release our emotions often mirrors the way we froze them. If you've been impatient, agitated, and demanding, it can feel that way when you're releasing these emotions. It's as though the emotions are going in reverse. Remember, though, it's just the melting of the past freezing. When you get a splinter in your finger, it goes in fast and quick. To get it out, you usually have to do some digging, and it has to come out the same way it went in. If it's really deep, now you have to cut down into it. Allowing it to release is a less invasive way of healing.

Sometimes releasing the emotions is like a stingray with a tail that has barbs, preventing it from going out the same way it went in. In this case, you have to find a way to either dissolve the barb or cut it out. If you allow your emotions to keep festering, they ultimately take form in the body and you eventually have to cut them out – as in cancer.

Being cooked softens the heart and opens it up to grace. At times, the heart's opening is not pretty, and the unfolding can get messy. It's usually manure that comes before the roses! If you notice that your reactivity is increasing, ask yourself if it might be your heart opening and releasing the old manure. If so, you're being prepared for the roses, so keep you heart open and keep moving forward. Usually it's other people in our lives that turn up the heat and help us with our releasing. Many times this is the process chosen by our teachers, because it works.

The movie *License to Wed* is a humorous example of being cooked and what happens when we stay open to all possibilities. In this film, Sadie Jones and Ben Murphy are getting married, but not until they go through the required training with their parish priest, Reverend Frank (Robin Williams). Reverend Frank turns up the temperature on this couple, and we get to see how it plays out. Sadie and Ben must pass a series of tests so Reverend Frank can determine whether they are ready for marriage. These tests turn up the heat in their relationship. Getting cooked sometimes feels like being tested. *License to Wed* is a humorous movie that shows what being cooked looks like for both the feminine and masculine traits.

Sadie tries to roll with it – pleasing, cajoling, and trying to keep the peace. This contrasts with Ben's reactivity of railing against the situation; he turns to anger to try to find a way to force the peace. As Reverend Frank says, "Someone once said that marriage is bliss, but that someone probably wasn't married." We get a good laugh at the opening of their hearts and how messy it gets. If only we could see our own lives and marriages from this humorous perspective, perhaps we could move through the cooking process more quickly.

Sometimes we make unreasonable promises in our relationships, such as Ben's promise in his vows "never to fart." In the end, Sadie and Ben get what they desire; it just doesn't look the way they thought it would.

What Are Two-by-Four Events?

Two-by-four events are the result of being cooked and not recognizing what is going on below the surface. The heat keeps getting turned up until you can no longer recognize the messages. It gets hotter and hotter until a two-by-four wake-up call happens. What do these events look like? Getting fired, divorce, health problems, car accidents, financial chaos, the loss of a friendship, etc. are common examples. These types of events happen because you've most likely been unaware and/or unavailable, and thus unable to read the signs or receive the feather-like guidance. These events often feel like they've come out of the blue, even though that's rarely the case. They're abrupt and always painful. If you are holding a rigid position with someone else or in response to an event that is occurring, when the two clash, you get a two-by-four moment.

Think about what happens when birds intersect with a plane's engine – both the bird and the jet lose, and it's messy. The birds and the plane are both oblivious to what is going on; each is moving at its own unique speed and direction and is unaware of what is about to happen. Once they intersect, both parties aren't flying anymore. This is a powerful two-by-four event.

Sue-Anne's second husband was totally caught by surprise when she asked for a divorce. She had done everything she could to resolve the problems, such as counseling, her own personal work, Linguistic Programming (NLP), etc. Yet somehow it was still a shock to him when she followed through with the divorce. This is a common response when a marriage ends. One partner is often caught totally off guard.

I Feel Like a Two-by-Four Just Hit Me – Now What Do I Do?

Don't panic. Stop and pause, stay out of action, slow down, and review what just happened. This is not the time go into reactive mode by taking action first and thinking later. See Foundation of Understanding chart on page 71.

Cinderella Man[53] is an example of how to respond to a two-by-four event. Jim Braddock (Russell Crow) and Mae Braddock (Renee Zellweger) lose everything in the Great Depression. They even come close to losing their children. The Braddocks were used to having all the luxuries life had to offer, only to lose it all.

In this movie, we observe how they deal with their loss and how they survive. With each turn of events, the Braddocks keep moving, taking one step at time. You don't see them focusing on the past or worrying about how to get back what they've lost. They're just trying to get through the day. When Jim decides to fight the heavyweight champion who was responsible for two men dying as a result of fighting with him, Mae doesn't think she can handle it. When they return home, her fears start to build; she envisions him being buried and her in black, the widow. As her fears mount, she has an outburst, saying she can't agree to it. Notice how Jim responds. He remains calm, doesn't become defensive, and just keeps quiet. This is how we can help each other when one of us is feeling emotional or having an outburst. It's another form of love and support that builds connection and intimacy.

When one person can stay centered like this, the one who is struggling is able to move through the situation more quickly, doesn't feel judged, and has a safe way out of the rut. Notice how Jim Braddock doesn't react to others' jabs and reporters' unfair questions. He doesn't try to defend himself but instead usually finds a clever way to disarm them. Jim and Mae persevere, overcoming their hardships and becoming stronger in the process.

Once Is Enough

Notice when you relive an experience over and over again through the retelling of it to friends, social networks, etc. Why make it worse by reactivating the pain every time? Wasn't the initial event painful enough? Sympathy from friends just numbs the pain temporarily. Don't make things worse by continually ranting about what should have happened or how you're a victim. The more you push against the event, the longer you stay in it, and the harder is for you.

Stop Beating a Dead Horse

Constantly replaying the past in your mind over and over again is just beating a dead horse. You'll end up experiencing more pain than the actual event. Mental connections are not logical – they are emotion-based and rarely the truth.

Look at what you feel and why you feel it. View the entire situation, along with the people involved. Many of us are inclined to take action and speak in public, trying to rally sympathetic support for our position. We tell as many friends as necessary to reinforce our feelings. This prolongs us being stuck where we are, and it just takes longer to get out of this groove. Remember, intensity simply deepens the groove. Take some time to discover your family beliefs, because there may be some answers waiting for you.

Surrender

Let go of the idea that you should have all the answers. Release the idea that you know what is true and acknowledge that you have only one perspective. Become aware that your thinking is limited to your current life experience. Be willing to give up your rigid truths. Remember, surrender does not mean submission. It's about releasing, letting go, and being peaceful in the face of the unknown. This allows the next best action to surface.

The Serenity Prayer by Reinhold Niebuhr[54] speaks to this in a modified version:

God, grant me the serenity to accept the things I cannot change; the courage to change the things that I can; and the wisdom to know the difference. Living one day at a time; enjoying one moment at a time; accepting hardships as a pathway to peace.

Give Up Your Attachments to Outcomes

Be open to all possibilities. Even what is happening right now is serving you. It's one of many possibilities, and apparently it's the best one for you in this moment and time.

Trust Your Process and Take Care of Yourself

Exercise, be mindful of what you're eating, consume foods that support your immune system, and get adequate rest.

Creation Can Look Chaotic

Chaos, which can also be called adversity, can be both a feather and a two-by-four. It is a sign that change is happening. Imagine a child playing with LEGOs. He builds something and then decides he wants something different. Usually, he tears it down so he can build something new, and he rarely cares how messy it might get. Especially for boys, the messier, the better. If you encounter chaos and adversity, know that it's just change and not something to resist. Examples of chaos or adversity in our lives can be everything from a water heater bursting or a change in jobs to a move to a new area or a divorce. In the extreme, it can be a natural disaster.

These events can be feathers trying to guide you. The more you can flow with a particular feather, the more it doesn't have to turn into a two-by-four event. Being able to flow with what is right in front of you keeps the event from becoming bigger. You really do have a choice about which way you want to go when you experience chaos and adversity. Do you want the feather, or do you want the drama of a two-by-four event? Regardless of your choice, the adversity will still continue – the key is how you choose to respond. The more you can be impermeable to the changes, chaos, and the adversity that's present, the more you can keep from sliding into the groove of fear and uncertainty. It's the sense of hope and optimism that helps you get through just about any life experience. When you can see chaos as neutral, then you can recognize that you have a choice to respond or react to it. If you can seek to understand how this is serving you, you can catch yourself from slipping into reactivity and take the steps to discern how you desire to respond. When you get emotional, this is change trying to serve you. Ask Jack Kornfield says, "Only to the extent that we let go into change can we live in harmony with those around us and our own true nature."

Why Don't We Take the Easy Way and Follow the Feathers?

The answer is that we usually get stuck in fear; we defer our emotions, thinking it will avoid pain. Fear is the expectation of pain.

When we anticipate pain, we add another layer. This leads to actually feeling pain that has not even happened yet. Think of how you feel on Sunday night. Your evening is spent focusing on how bad you'll feel on Monday, consuming your Sunday night and making the pain worse than just experiencing it in real time. Somehow you think that if you can feel the pain now, you'll be able to mitigate it for tomorrow. However, it just doesn't work that way, so you end up intensifying it. You have to stop anticipating tomorrow's pain. Tomorrow isn't here yet, and you can't truly experience it until it gets here. So why try to live there now? We get stuck in our heads trying to spend tomorrow's money or next month's money now. It's just not possible to pay next month's bills until next month, so why do we worry about paying them when we won't have access to that money until next month?

"Future pain is to be avoided – stop doing the things that are causing the pain. Suffering which is yet to come can be avoided."[55]
– Patanjali, Yoga Sutras, 2.16

We Defer Our Pain

Many of us turn to prescription drugs to cover our emptiness and our emotional pain. When we're sick, we take something to lower the fever instead of allowing the body to do its thing. Pills have become a socially accessible way to not hurt for us – and for our children. According to Dr. Oz, pain serves us and helps us to see what is causing the pain. "In the US, we have a need or desire to run from pain, instead of look at it… we hide from our problems, our need or desire to run from the pain. More people abuse prescription drugs in the US than cocaine, heroin, and ecstasy combined."[56]

We avoid pain by telling stories we think will please ourselves and our loved ones. In the long run, this doesn't work and kills intimacy. We continue to prop up how we really feel or how things are really going in our lives by telling people that everything is fine when it's not. We don't tell those closest to us the truth because we think it might hurt them. We don't want to cause a fuss, thinking this is how we support each other. We can only prop up these lies for so long until a two-by-four event uncovers the truth.

In the movie *Everybody's Fine,*[57] Frank Goode (Robert De Niro) finally realizes that his children, his wife, and he himself have been glossing over everything as being fine. A year after Frank's wife dies, he goes on a surprise journey to visit each of his children. What he learns from the trip is that his children are not telling him what is really going on with their lives. Frank sees that, in many ways, he doesn't know them anymore. A facade has been perpetuated by everyone, and it takes three major events to uncover truth: Frank's wife dies, he has a heart attack, and he discovers the truth of what happened to his son. This experience is a wake-up call to Frank. Finally, he starts to insist that his children tell him what is really going on. Frank confesses to his children that for forty-two years he didn't have the heart to tell his wife that she had been overcooking the turkey at Christmastime. Ironically, Frank's spouse may have thought that she was cooking it just the way he liked it.

Our goal is to make nice with the pain. When you cooperate with the pain, you accept it as it is, and this gives you more opportunities to see the feather that is trying to guide you. If you will look at the pain when it first happens, you'll have more chance of addressing it easily, and this helps to quickly move thought it. When you resist it, the pain gets deferred for another time, takes longer to move, and usually is worse than the initial pain. Deferring the pain opens you up to more forceful guidance, and if you don't look at it, your choices of responding or healing get taken away – hence the two-by-four effect.

We Defer Our Joy, Too

We don't celebrate the little things, the little moments. It's all about doing – there's no time to just enjoy this moment and make the most of what is already here. Many of us postpone joy and celebration until retirement. Many hard-charging businessmen reach retirement, and then they die.

Sometimes retirement plans don't work out like we expect. We push ourselves and give 150 percent to our jobs and businesses. We plan to discover joy in our life once we've "made it," but until then we just have to work harder. Sometimes we don't make it to retirement, or our life takes other twists we don't expect.

In the movie *After the Wedding*,[58] we see this all-too-common pattern play out. Jorgen Hanson is a highly successful CEO who decides to make a donation to an orphanage in India. Mr. Hanson lives on an estate outside Copenhagen, Denmark. He's a big and powerful man who lives life to the fullest. He has put all his energy into his business. He appears to have it all: wealth, power, a beautiful spouse, and ample money for his altruistic projects.

We learn, however, that Jorgen is missing one key component that his money can't buy: his health. This movie has several twists and turns that we'll allow you to discover. However, we do want you to see that Jorgen's power and money couldn't buy the health he needed to survive. He was so successful in business that he probably assumed he would be able to enjoy the fruits of his labor during retirement. So many of us just keep working harder, hoping we'll get to enjoy life once we're retired. It really seems like a race to the finish. Sometimes the finish line isn't what we expected, and it's too late to go back and recapture the joy we deferred.

We Don't Want to Be Vulnerable

Vulnerability is strength. We think that that being vulnerable will open us up to pain. However, the goal is to be vulnerable while remaining peaceful. Being vulnerable in relationships opens the heart and makes it available for intimate connections with others. An open heart is our true nature; it takes energy to keep us from being vulnerable.

Remaining vulnerable in relationships can become another overture to peace of mind. Overtures aren't always perfect – most are actually clumsy. Whether musical, political, or relational, we all have examples of overtures that weren't perfect. If we would just let go and not worry about messing up, we would make deeper connections with others, but many times we're too afraid that we'll screw up.

Connection with another person when both of you are vulnerable is a real-time give-and-take of energy that creates something new outside of you. It takes strength to be vulnerable and surrender to your own unpredictable nature and other people's response to it. The more you practice this while remaining peaceful, the easier it gets, and peace of mind becomes more of a way of life while in community with others.

In the book *Kansas Troubles* by Earlene Fowler, Benni thinks of her first marriage to Jack. "One of the most comforting and fulfilling aspects of my relationship with Jack had been the complete openness between us, something I realize now I'd taken for granted. That kind of emotional intimacy came much easier when you were fifteen and eager to have every little feeling and experience. When connecting with another person at the halfway point in your lives, discoveries are made much more slowly and with more hesitation."[59]

Perhaps as we get older we think we have more to lose, and so we feel like we have to hold back parts of ourselves. We think by now we should have it together, and it's embarrassing to reveal that we don't. Ironically, we hold back with the people we're sharing our lives with, afraid to expose these sides of ourselves.

In Tyler Perry's movie *Why Did I Get Married?*,[60] we see how four couples resist being vulnerable with their mates and with each other. These eight college friends are best friends that get together annually for vacation and to rekindle their friendships. This year's meeting is at a ski lodge in Colorado. During their vacation, secrets are revealed, and each couple begins to question their own marriage dynamic. The themes that play out are very real and common in most relationships. All four couples resist staying vulnerable and open to their mates. We see how this affects their relationships, and how demanding expectations of each other can be. We set such high standards and rules, it's no wonder we resist being vulnerable to our mates.

We Rationalize What Is Happening to Maintain Our Picture

We tell ourselves rational lies. We defer our pain by making up stories and, as a result, the emotion that is trying to be expressed remains in the body. There's nothing wrong with positive, better-feeling stories. But there's a difference between painting over our feelings and trying to reach for better feelings up the continuum.

Does this mean that you shouldn't embrace positive thinking? No, but you should only presume that positive thinking will gradually move you through the emotions. Otherwise, you simply defer the emotions for another time.

For example, you can't paint over mold on the walls of your house and still live there without an impact on your system. Even our bodies heal from the inside out. Think of this in respect to the emotions – you have to heal from within before it can show in your outer life. When you continue to create rational lies, you miss the feather guidance and set yourself up for bigger problems – possibly two-by four wake-up calls.

In the movie *Solitary Man*,[61] Ben Kalmen's life goes into chaos after learning he may have heart problems. At the time, Ben (Michael Douglas) is a successful car dealer in a long-term marriage who appears to be on top of the world. The news from his doctor is so jarring to Ben that he refuses to take the tests to see what's going on with his heart. Instead, he leaves the doctor's office and goes into a downward spiral that lasts for the next six-and-a-half years of his life. During this period, he avoids the tests and pretends that nothing is wrong.

Ben Kalmen's experience is a common response that many men have later in life. At some point, they accomplish much in business and then get a wake-up call that reminds them of life's impermanence. Ben starts to feel invisible and sees his power and influence slipping away. Just the thought of allowing a doctor to tell him he has health issues makes Ben feel that too much of his power is being taken away. As a result, he'd rather not know what the tests would reveal. We see how Ben rationalizes his choices and reactively goes from one day to the next, grasping for power in anyway he can find it.

Ben thinks he will regain his power by cheating on his business, his wife, and his family. He's no longer invisible, but he's now lost all the good will that once was a part of the life that made him feel so powerful. His conquests become addictive and unconscious. He's not really aware of what has happened to him. In the end, Ben Kalmen gets another chance to create a new way of living. He's lived most of his life from external power and is now given a chance at inner authentic power: accepting himself for who he is and where he is in his life.

We Don't Want to Ask for Help

When a woman experiences pain, she is more likely to reach out to other women for assistance. On the other hand, men have a tendency to stay in their caves so they don't appear weak; they stuff the pain or self-medicate. However, asking for help is not a sign of weakness – it's a sign of strength. When men are in pain or struggling, they tend to just keep pushing harder. Instead of finding ways to work smarter, they keep hoping that more hard work will solve the problem. Men don't want to look within.

We Slip Back into Unconscious Reactivity

In the movie *The Burning Plain*,[62] a young women's reactivity changes both her own life and her mother's. It leads to a two-by-four event that she doesn't anticipate. Reactivity is unconscious but not necessarily instantaneous. It blinds you to the implications of what you are doing. There are always effects from all our actions, and this movie shows how they play out and how those effects grow with time. While the pain is deferred, it gets more complicated over time. However, there are still opportunities to recognize what's really happening if you will pause and look. Then you can respond differently.

Remember, when you've slipped into one of these reactive roles, you lose your perception. It's similar to falling through thin ice and being disoriented by the freezing water. You are now in survival mode, and others jumping in with you just keeps you there longer. Sometimes we think we're being loving when we join others in their distress, but real love is holding people in their greatness and not matching where they are emotionally. When someone falls through the ice, you throw them a line, a ladder, a stick – anything from solid ground. Going out on the ice to save them puts you in peril and takes them longer to get out. It also can deepen the groove, or rut, for the other person.

In *Notting Hill*,[63] there is a scene that provides an example of how you support people in their greatness. William Thacker (Hugh Grant) is telling his friends how he responded to Anna Scott's (Julia Roberts) overtures to reconnect with him. When he tells his friends what he said, they don't answer him and let him figure out that maybe he missed something. Staying quiet has more of an impact on William because he finally gets it himself.

When you recognize that someone has slipped into a reactive mode or a lifetime groove, think of yourself as the Starship Enterprise from Star Trek. Keeping yourself centered allows you to put out a tractor-beam, if you will, of love. Just like the Starship Enterprise, your powerful vibrations will pull others in and give them the support they need. You'll do more for others if you can support them from this place than if you join them in their reactivity. Love is the most powerful force in the Universe, so why not beam it out?

In the movie *What Dreams May Come,*[64] Christy (Robin Williams) joins his wife in her hell. We see how she created her own unique hell, and trying to get her out becomes a perilous quest. As the Tracker warns Christy, "You were expecting physical danger? What could it do, kill ya, huh? No, in hell there's real danger… of losing your mind." This movie is a good example of how we think we serve others by joining them. On the contrary, it usually takes them longer, and there is a risk you will get stuck with them.

The Tracker tries to warn Christy, "We'll find her. But when you find her, nothing will make her recognize you. Nothing will break her denial. It's stronger than her love. In fact, it's reinforced by her love. You can say everything you long to say, including good-bye, even if she can't understand it, and you'll have the satisfaction that you didn't give up. That has to be enough." Christy believes that, because of his love, he has to save her, even if it means being stuck in his wife's self-created hell. Remember, love is holding people in their greatness and not matching them where they are emotionally. ▣

✖ CHAPTER SUMMARY ✖

It's been said that experience creates wisdom. When we look back at our lives, we can see that even the two-by-four events were experiences that provided wisdom. When we can follow the feathers in our life, we'll flow through our experiences with much more grace and ease. We will then be able to see that life is supposed to be joyful. It just depends on whether we want the feathers to guide us — or the two-by-fours.

BELIEF STATEMENTS REPRESENTED IN THIS CHAPTER:

Energizing Beliefs

❖ I communicate clearly and openly.

❖ I am forgiven and I forgive.

❖ I let go of my traumas and allow my heart to heal.

❖ I can respond and don't have to slip into reactivity.

❖ I have a role in this country and find out how I can contribute.

❖ I forgive myself for the way I treated my man/woman.

❖ Everything always works out for me.

❖ I know when to let up.

❖ My gentleness with my spouse helps us communicate and understand each other better.

❖ I flow with my life and let go of my resistance to change.

❖ I respect other people's journeys and know that they have a direction to be honored.

❖ I now only want to uplift myself and others.

❖ I see affirmations of life all around me.

❖ I appreciate all of my life experiences.

❖ I always have a second chance to find new connections with my family.

❖ I appreciate my mate's willingness to grow with me.

❖ I keep my heart open and desire deeper connections with my mate and others.

❖ I appreciate the lessons I've learned from my marriage and don't regret the experience.

❖ When my marriage is not going well, I reach out for help.

De-energizing Beliefs

❖ My children have no respect for me.

❖ I can't say no, so I have to avoid anyone that makes me uncomfortable.

❖ I'm afraid of getting old.

❖ I'm uncomfortable with anyone who is not like me.

❖ People never change.

❖ All is fair in love, war, and politics.

❖ I have to be smart and look the other way even if I know it's wrong.

❖ I don't have any power to defend myself.

❖ My career is first; children and family can wait.

❖ I'm angry because everything and everyone in my world is against me.

❖ If people love me, they'll do what I say and be obedient.

❖ I expect my mate to take over when things get tough.

❖ I'm so afraid things won't work out for me and my mate.

❖ I'm number one and nothing else matters.

❖ I have helped others succeed, but when I need support, they forget what I did for them.

❖ I don't think I can handle another disappointment.

❖ I'm paranoid of people with money and think they always have an ulterior motive.

❖ I don't know how to talk and connect with others.

❖ I can't see how my behavior is isolating me.

❖ I have to tell people what to do whether they ask for my advice or not.

❖ I am supposed to be the strong one for my spouse and loved ones.

❖ I don't want to look at the pain in my life and would rather get lost in my work.

❖ It's too late for me — my children are grown-up and they don't need me anymore.

❖ If I'm vulnerable and open to my mate, I'll be betrayed.

❖ My mate needs to change before I can be happy.

MUSIC SELECTIONS

"Moment of Surrender," U2

"That's the Truth," George Strait

"There's Hope," India Arie

"Let Him Fly" Dixie Chicks

Mozart Piano Concerto No. 23 in A major K488: Adagio

ESSENTIAL OIL RECOMMENDATIONS

Dill: Calms the autonomic nervous system with a spicy, fresh scent that is stimulating, revitalizing, and balancing.

Marjoram: Has a warming affect on both mind and body. It is beneficial for occasional simple nervous tension. Marjoram was known as the "herb of happiness" to the Romans and "joy of the mountains" to the Greeks.

Tarragon: Helps you digest whatever is going on in your world.

Acceptance: Stimulates the mind, compelling it to open and accept new things in life. This blend also helps to overcome procrastination and denial.

Motivation: Stimulates feelings of action and accomplishment, providing positive energy to help overcome feelings of fear and procrastination.

CHAPTER 6

The Fire of Passion

Passion is defined as any strong feeling or emotion. Usually we think of passion as limited to sexual feelings or rage. Rarely do we see that it applies to all emotions. Passion is an intensity, a very strong feeling about a person or thing, or an abandoned display of emotion. Passion is similar to the intensity of fire.

Fire burns and creates new life. Similar to the phoenix rising, you burn the dross and allow the light to come forth. This is the way passion operates in our lives. Fire describes what passion does. Passion engulfs whatever it's focused on. You add heat, and this allows it to change form. The passion itself is a form of fire.

The fire of passion allows you to burn through things. When you're in a passionate state there is no room for the idea that you could fail. Have you ever been so lost in some activity that you become completely absorbed in it? It's as if you've become one with the activity, a type of union. The heart and mind are completely absorbed – that's the fire of passion.

Think of passion in terms of the emotional system. It has the same effect as fire does in this earthly world in that it allows itself to be transmuted. Think of the two-headed dragon, Devon and Cornwall, in the movie *Quest for Camelot*.[65] Once Devon and Cornwall got their emotions working, all the parts, then they could be at peace with the entire emotional range. As a result, they could then move into a place of being passionate about even their emotional state. Before, Devon and Cornwall disliked each other greatly. They couldn't fly or breathe fire. Now they could use their emotional state as a fire, giving them the ability to physically produce it, whereas in the past all they could produce was powerless and feeble puffs.

Passion can produce a result that heats or brings light to wherever it is focused. The fire of summer can temper the letting go inherent in fall. Sue-Anne has witnessed how this plays out in her hospice work, as she assists both those grieving and those dying. Often the primary caregiver is immersed in a deep well of letting go. It is the connection, love, and passion of those around them that helps these caregivers to let go and release their grief. It's not uncommon to see a caregiver reaching out for a passionate connection to someone else to relieve the burden of letting go.

Unfortunately, we judge this harshly, even though it's an understandable way of summer making way for fall. In the movie *Eyes Wide Shut*,[66] Dr. William "Bill" Hartford (Tom Cruise) is called to the deathbed of a friend's father. When he arrives to console her, she tries to initiate sex with Dr. Bill while her father is still lying in the bed. This may look distorted, but it's not an uncommon occurrence in this context.

Fire is neutral – it isn't good or bad. The point is how you use it. When harnessed, it creates light, warmth, and assists in transformation, land, food, metals, etc. Before the invention of electricity, fire kept us alive. Fire is necessary and can bring us much comfort. When left untamed, it can do great harm; it can destroy entire forests and homes and even cause death. We all know what to do with fire and what not to do. When you cooperate with fire, it brings you what you desire.

If you're passionate about something, you know you are completely aligned with it and have no doubt for the good, bad, and the ugly. You're in the zone and you know it. This becomes a powerful union wherever you focus your fire of passion.

Be Clear on the Intention Directing Your Passion

See your intention as the way you harness your own passion. Think of going on a hot-air balloon ride. The basket stays on the ground until you ignite the fire that fills the balloon with hot air. The fire is our passion that fuels our intention, which creates movement towards our desires. This passion allows us to lift off the ground, and our intention or goal sets the direction. It isn't our passion that misguides us – it's what we do with it. As with fire, if you're not clear with how you use fire, you can burn down a forest. Additionally, fire can be unpredictable, so before you unleash it, you'd better be clear on how you want to use it.

When you are passionate about something, you allow for considered right action. Don't confuse frenetic energy with passion.

Frenetic means that you throw everything at your goal. It's like a spinning ball hoping for a strike wherever it hits. Passion, at its best, means that you have laser-pointed activity that absorbs you, and there's no perception of separation from it.

Focused Passion Has Lasting Effects

The movie *The Red Violin*[67] is an example of what happens when you focus your passions. Nicolo Bussotti's passionate love for his family goes into creating a beautiful red-colored violin for his soon-to-be born son. He's so immersed in the making of the violin, it's as if it consumes him. Busssotti's focus becomes mixed with his desire for perfection, along with his incredible heartbreak when his wife unexpectedly dies in childbirth. The violin becomes a representation of passionate intentions all over the world and throughout time. Nicolo's intent for this instrument continues to resonate for hundreds of years.

When the violin becomes simply an object to be owned because of its monetary value, it stirs corresponding values in people and they act accordingly to acquire it. Each person associated with the violin was extremely passionate about it for his or her own reasons. We get to see how the original intention plays out with each owner or player of the violin. Each person is consumed by the passion the violin represents, the desire to attain musical perfection through playing or owning it. This passion becomes all-consuming and ends in heartbreak, just as it did for its original creator, Nicolo Bussotti. The energy of our intentions can stir passions and ripple out longer and further than we're aware. Yes, this energy can be boundless, and that's why you need to be clear about your intent.

When you consciously build passion for light or love, you have more opportunities to respond with choice than from reactivity.

There Are Many Objects of Passion

When someone says they're passionate about something, we think we know what they mean. Usually we don't, unless we know their intent. The intent is usually focused on an object or a thing: a lover, a hobby, a sport, a job, a family, etc. To explain this further, we have chosen three common objects of passion: love, sex, and money.

Love as an Object

We think of love as merely an emotion or erotic passion. What we've lost is the understanding that love is selflessness based on action. Instead, we confuse love with an infatuation based on attachment. Once we think we're in love, or attached, we want our mate to adhere to a whole set of conditional rules that are more about ownership and less about love. We think that getting attached, or being in love, means that we get to own our mate's past and future love experiences. This type of ownership leads to a passion that can get out of control when others don't live up to our definitions of love and commitment. We picture love as a paradise without conflict or problems, but true love is an active choice that we keep making over and over again. Like peace, it isn't a destination that you arrive at and stay forever more. It's a choice you continue to make every day.

The movie *Love Trap*[68] begins with Richard's thoughts on love: "We spend so much of our time trying to find love... this feeling in my heart that wonders how I got from there to here." When Richard (Julius Golden) is propositioned by a flashy and beautiful woman, he doesn't just reactively accept. He seeks advice, and then decides how he wants to respond. He doesn't merely react and allow his passion to overtake him. He slows down, puts a plan in place, and takes action from a place of love.

Sex as an Object

Throughout history, passion has become synonymous with sex. Passion has been mistaken as reactive sexuality. If sexual expression is reactive and unthinking, we think it must be true, unbridled passion. In fact, some believe that if they don't feel this way about their mate, there isn't any passion. We believe this is a distortion of passion and liken it more to seeing sex as an object. When sex is an object, it's usually a reactivity that's unconscious. By contrast, when our sexual energies are focused from love, sex becomes more heart-based, a response to love. This creates a powerful union between two people, where each is completely absorbed.

De-Lovely[69] is a biographical movie about Cole Porter (played by Kevin Klein). Cole Porter shows us what sex as an object looks like and how it conflicts with the heartfelt love and bond he has with his wife Linda (Ashley Judd). We see how Cole's choices affect Linda, leaving him sad, lonely, in pain, and full of regret. Cole Porter was a passionate man, and his musical genius filled the world with joy and entertainment. His music is still beloved today.

In the beginning of the movie, Cole has died and is looking back at his life with his guardian angel, Gabe. We see the highs and lows of his life, the choices he made and what he has regretted. Cole Porter had it all, but he lost his passion for music, love, and even for his life. He regretted how his sexual expression hurt his beloved wife Linda. Even though Linda understood him like nobody could, he couldn't forgive himself for being who he was and the choices he made. He spent his last years lonely and sad. This is a touching movie, and if you're a Cole Porter fan, you'll enjoy it. The acting and music is superb. And it delivers a strong message about how our reactive sexual drives can do more harm than just hurting the ones we love.

In the movie *Unfaithful*,[70] we see how using sex as an object can put us in dangerous situations. It can get out control, leading to harm and even death. Connie Sumner (Diane Lane) decides to engage in an affair outside her marriage. It's exciting for her, but she doesn't anticipate how it will affect her husband, Ed (Richard Gere), when he discovers the truth about her secret affair. Connie probably didn't play out all the scenarios that might happen when she dove into her experience. Things get out of control, changing her life and Ed's forever.

Think of the uncontained fire example earlier in this chapter. When fire is not harnessed, it can cause great destruction. Things can get dicey when our sex drive is reactive and causes us to step out against our cultural belief systems that center around love and commitment.

Sex as an object is a big subject that could take several books to fully explore. It's such a deep groove on our planet. Sex has had a distorting affect on both men and women, as well as on our understanding of love – not to mention how this groove has impacted entire industries that profit and exploit others in harmful ways. It's no wonder many of us don't want to look at this area of our lives. It seems dirty, or it can be perceived as a dark aspect of being human.

Our erroneous beliefs about sex can then have another impact when we deny this side of ourselves and try to bury it.

In Stanley Kubrick's film *Eyes Wide Shut,*[71] we see what can occur when we repress our sexual expression. Dr. Bill Harford (Tom Cruise) is married to Alice Harford (Nicole Kidman). When Bill learns that Alice almost had an affair and has fantasies that don't include him, he becomes obsessed with going out and finding his own experience. First, he engages with a prostitute but changes his mind at the last minute. Next, he is invited to a clandestine party of masked people engaged in ritualistic orgies. Bill quickly realizes that he's in over his head; he becomes aware of the danger he's in and how it could harm his family.

When we repress our sexual desires, this energy is going to find ways to get out. It can be expressed as fantasies, voyeurism, etc. Fantasies are not bad if they bring couples together. Fantasies serve if they support and help you connect with your primary relationship.

However, if you are focusing on someone else, you are not present with your partner, and this keeps you from connecting in deeper, more intimate ways. *Eyes Wide Shut* shows that a purely animalistic response to sex is faceless, impersonal, and many times not what we think it might be. You might be looking for your mind and emotions to be stimulated – something erotic. But because you're not connecting with anything else but another person's body, you don't get a mind, body, and soul experience. Instead, it's a one-dimensional physical experience. We all want passion to involve the body, mind, and soul, and this is just not possible with nameless, faceless partners. As Dr. David Schnarch says, "There's no beauty in sex – the beauty

is in people. You can't save the beauty in sex, you have to put it in....
Sex becomes beautiful when we bring our personal beauty to it."[72]

Money as an Object

Over the centuries of human history, money has become an
object of passion that has engulfed countless individuals and entire
societies. As a result, we've created many erroneous beliefs about
money. To many of us, it's the source of all evil, while others insist it's
necessary to retain power. Money is no longer simply a form to be
utilized as an exchange between humans – we've made it so much
more. We may not realize that we've turned money into an object of
passion, and thus many of us get consumed by it. Remember, when
you're passionate about something, you become consumed by it, and
a type of union occurs.

In India, for thousands of years the Ganges River has been
considered to be sacred. Hindus have worshiped it as the goddess
Ganga. This belief has been practiced by countless humans who
passionately believe in its sacred energy and power. Great mahatmas
have brought their passionate love, devotion, faith, and blessings to
this river. As a result, it *is* sacred: many are healed by it, and there is
nothing anyone can say or try to disprove it otherwise.

The birthplace of Francis of Assisi is another example of how
spiritual passions create tangible sacred sites in the world. St. Francis is
a beloved Catholic friar from the thirteenth century. He has become
such an inspiration to people around the world that they make
pilgrimages to Assisi to visit where Francis lived. Because so many
humans bring their passionate devotion, faith, and love to Assisi each

year, it too has become a sacred site. Because we passionately believe it is, so it is.

We use these two examples as how passion applies to money. Think of what each of us bring to money every time we come into contact with it. We bring all our erroneous thoughts, fears, and attachments to this thing we call money. These powerful energies have a tangible effect on it. If this is true, we've created it to be something it doesn't have to be. Just like the Ganges River and Assisi, Italy, our collective energies have transformed money. When you make money an object of passion, you become absorbed by it, and a tangible union occurs.

In the movie *There Will Be Blood*,[73] Daniel Plainview is a charismatic oilman. He's passionate about acquiring as much oil as possible. His ruthless tactics catch many by surprise, including himself. There's nothing he won't do to accumulate more. His passion for power and money engulf him, and he's not even aware of it. His intent becomes money at all costs. This passion becomes destructive to Daniel and others. He becomes alienated, and we see how it affects his life.

In *Brewster's Millions*,[74] Montgomery Brewster (Richard Pryor) has to spend $30 million in thirty days so he can inherit $300 million. Brewster is not allowed to acquire assets, nor can he tell anyone why he's spending so much money. It's humorous to see how difficult this task can be for Brewster. Like all of us, he initially believes that having money will solve all his problems and then he'll be happy. He learns this is not the case. After successfully meeting the challenge, Brewster has a new awareness of money. This new understanding prepares him for receiving his vast inheritance.

Money is certainly a big topic, and we've barely touched on it here. For now, think about your own beliefs around money. What are you willing to do for it? Is acquiring more money your passion? How does the acquisition of money affect your life, your relationships, and your other passions? Be aware of your thought and energies whenever you spend money. Are you reactive about money? Can you be at peace with what you have in this moment?

Ways That We Squelch Our Passions

Many times we squelch our passions before they ever have a chance to take off. It's a type of self-sabotage that limits our life experience and keeps us from following our dreams. Like stepping on your own dragon tail, it keeps you from flying. Doubt and fear are two ways we squelch our passion.

Doubt Throws a Blanket on the Fire

Have you ever met a dreamer – someone who gets so excited about his/her ideas, someone who desires to experience life in a grand way and see the world? And yet, for this type of dreamer, there's always a reason why their dream can't be realized. Maybe you know someone like this, or maybe this could be speaking to you. Many times it's doubt that keeps the dreamer's ideas in the ethers. The many facets of doubt prevent their passions from being realized. Just when the fire of their passion is ignited, doubt acts as a wet blanket and smothers it before it takes off.

A common facet of doubt is the belief that something better is on the way, so you'll just wait and see what happens. Just when a decision requires a time or financial commitment, this facet of doubt tricks you into believing that the grass is greener, requiring more research, more dreaming. This can also be seen in relationships, when you doubt whether you've found the right mate or not.

Another facet of doubt is the belief that your passion and dream isn't worthy of achieving. Maybe it's a business idea that thrills you, but you think that no one will agree with you so you don't try to sell your idea to investors. It could be the desire to write the next great novel, but you don't think you're a good enough writer, so what's the point in trying? Doubt has clever ways of distracting you from your dreams.

Some people doubt they'll be successful because they have a type of "poverty consciousness." They've never experienced real financial freedom, and they can't imagine ever getting out of the shackles of day-to-day sustenance. As a result, they just give up because they don't have the money. It can be a mindset that says, "Our family has always struggled with money, and so must I... it's just the way of the world." Or "My family is counting on me to provide a steady income, and I can't give that up to pursue my passions. I have to make money, and that's just the way it is."

A similar facet can be a belief that says, "If my dream worked, I'd be rich. This would then mean that I've sold out and now don't care about the world." We have many erroneous beliefs around money and people that have it.

Fear Blows Out the Fire

Fear is such a destructive force when it comes to realizing our dreams and passions – it acts like a strong wind that blows out the fire. Fear even keeps us from dreaming. We are afraid of failing in our endeavor. We fear the change it may have on our marriages or jobs. We're afraid of what others will think of us if we walk away from a career and go to cooking school. Some of us are afraid of having a public life. Fear also tricks us into thinking we're not good enough to realize our passion. This lack of confidence prevents us from taking any action and our fire is smothered before it ever had a chance to burn.

What to Do About Doubt and Fear?

Doubt and fear are indeed clever ways to keep us from realizing our passions in life. When you realize that these emotions distract you from attaining the intent you desire, they don't seem quite so clever. Distraction and reactivity will be present whenever you embark on some new passion. We experienced these twin emotions many times during the writing of this book. We discovered that when we are aware of them, staying focused on our dream and the tasks at hand works.

Focus is a powerful tool when you're trying to create anything new. First, it prevents delays when you recognize doubt and fear are messing with you. Second, and most important, focus gives you feedback on what's working and what's not, so you can adjust. As Steven Covey says, "You're going to be off track 90 percent of the time. So what? It's like the flight of an airplane... during the course of the flight, wind, rain, turbulence, air traffic, human error, and other factors act upon the plane... so most of the time the plane is not even on the prescribed flight plan."[75] While Mr. Covey uses this analogy to speak of families, we believe it works for any passion where there's a vision and a plan. It's about your ability to recognize the signs and get back to the flight plan that keeps you on course.

Diversity Fosters Passion... If We Let It

Every person is unique, with special gifts and insights to offer the world. We sometimes look at people that are not like us in age, experience, gender, race, religion, etc., as being limited in what they have to offer, or we think they are suspect. We misunderstand that each unique perspective can inspire new ideas, solve unresolved problems, and create new ways that benefit all of us. We are inclined to become set in our ways, and we cling to our own perspective of the world as the right one. Diverse groups can solve just about any problem, because they bring different perspectives that provide contrast for each of us. If we can stay open, this contrast can spark a fire that when harnessed can be very powerful.

When we all have the same experience, background, and history, we usually see obstacles and solutions in similar ways. Because we haven't been exposed to any other perspective, we don't know what we don't know.

In the movie *Unstoppable*,[76] a half-mile-long train, unmanned and traveling at high speeds, will surely cause a great disaster when it arrives in Stanton, Pennsylvania. Frank Barnes (Denzel Washington) and Will Colson (Chris Pine) develop a strategy that could possibly stop the train and save the town. Frank Barnes has been with the rail company for over twenty years; he's a seasoned veteran with valuable knowledge of all the facets of running a train. By all definitions, Frank is an expert. His knowledge and instincts are tested and reliable, and he's a valued employee. He's paired with Will Colson, a young man just starting his first day on the job. Will knows all the rules and regulations and gets to play them out on this first thrilling day.

The man that created the runaway train problem in the first place doesn't seem to take his supervisor, a young African-American woman, seriously. He doesn't respect her, calling her a "ballbuster." This man doesn't take the time to follow the rules because he just wants to get his supervisor off his back. Perhaps his resentment is due to the fact that she's the boss and he's not, or the fact that she's a woman. Whatever the reason, he gets reactive and takes careless shortcuts.

Throughout the movie, last minute decisions need to be made by Frank, Will, and many others on how best to stop this train. The solution comes when the key players stay open to new ideas and the changing situation. We see how diverse backgrounds in experience, gender, age, and race create scenarios that reveal a winning solution. Passions are stirred in each person on the team. The crisis is so fast and intense, no one has the luxury to be annoyed by another's differing perspective. All ideas have to be discerned and discussed, and choices must be made immediately. When we allow diversity to thrive unbridled, new ideas and passions are ignited in ways that can help everyone succeed. Each person gets to shine in their own unique brilliance, and we all benefit.

Be Open to Diverse Experiences

Living by a rigid set of rules, your emotional experience becomes limited and lacks passion. We tend to think there is a success formula to life that, if we follow it, will lead to happiness. As we set out on our individual paths, we have a tendency to slip into routines and our lives seem like they're on autopilot. We go to work, pay the bills, attend family functions, and do it all over again, day after day. It happens so fast that many of us don't recognize the limitation of our life experiences and how it leads to dissatisfaction. We can get so stuck that we're willing to do anything to escape how we feel and what's not working.

We see this portrayed in the movie *City Slickers*.[77] Mitch Robbins (Billy Crystal) goes on a two-week vacation, driving cattle from New Mexico to Colorado. His two friends, Phil and Ed, have given Mitch this trip as a gift for his thirty-ninth birthday. They've been taking similar adventures together for many years, but this year, their annual adventure takes on another meaning. All three men are at a period in their lives where they want to escape, and each one has tried his own way of doing it. Mitch isn't happy at work, and he tries to escape with cynical humor. Phil has a difficult marriage dynamic, and he escapes by having an affair with a young employee at his father-in-law's grocery store. Ed is trying to escape from his childhood and the fear that he may end up like his father. They all hope this trip will give them some relief.

When our emotions are telling us to look at an area of our life that no longer works, trying to escape from our issues can be problematic. It can just prolong the issues or create more problems. As Curly (Jack Palance), the trail boss, says to Mitch, "You spend about fifty weeks a year getting knots in your rope, and then you think two weeks up here will untie them for ya… none of ya get it."

This feeling of wanting to escape is a sign that it's time for you to discover something new in your life. Your passions have been squelched in some way. If your life consists of the same routine, how do you figure this out? We suggest that you try some new experiences outside of anything you've every done before. These new experiences will provide you with a contrast that will spark new ideas and inspiration. Ideally, you'll meet new people with different life experiences and cultures in places that are totally new. It's this contrast that refreshes your life. It helps you rediscover new and existing passions.

While on the trail, Curly asks Mitch if he knows the secret of life. Curly says, "One thing... just one thing. You stick to that, and everything else don't mean shit." Mitch, Phil, and Ed don't understand what Curly is trying to teach them. When Curly dies on the trail, the vacationing cowboys are thrown into crisis. Without his leadership, they descend into chaos. First, the hired hands get drunk and recklessly leave the cattle to fend for themselves. Doubt and fear grip Mitch, Phil, and Ed, and they just want to give up. However, Phil and Ed decide to try and lead the herd to Colorado. At the time it seems crazy, but they give it a try and commit to seeing it through.

This crisis creates an opportunity for the best of the three of them to be revealed. Each one has something unique they can contribute. They get pushed past their self-imposed limitations and rediscover their inner strength. Bringing in the herd becomes a thrilling experience for the three friends, and each returns home passionate for life again. Their own "one thing," what they value most, is revealed, and Curly's wisdom lives on.

Ways We Suppress Our Passions

At times, we squash our passions and this keeps from realizing our desires. We've identified three ways of being that can act like a fog to prevent us from experiencing our passions: We cling to our rules, we become attached to past pleasure, and we get stuck in past suffering.

We Cling to Our Rules

Many of us believe we have to adhere to a set of rules, be it family, cultural, religious, or political. These ways of being are tried and true. There's great pressure to adhere to these rules. Some of us never break free from them, and this limits our experience.

A Serious Man[78] and *Babette's Feast*[79] are both movie examples of narrow perspectives due to an adherence of the rules of community. These movies show clearly how limiting our choices can be when we lack diversity. As a result, our solutions to problems get limited too. Additionally, any new experiences of joy and celebration get squashed.

The Coen brothers' movie *A Serious Man* tells the story of Larry Gopnik, a man who is going through a significant life change. His world is coming apart at the seams, and Larry turns to advisors within his community for answers. While each tries to help him, all he seems to get are platitudes. Larry's world is in chaos, and there doesn't seem to be anyone that can provide real answers to his problems. Larry wants to discover new meaning in life, but he just keeps getting the same answers, and his awareness becomes limited.

We continue to cling to our traditions because this is what we've always valued. Change is an opportunity to discover new inner, albeit dormant, perspectives. Sometimes you need to break away from your current environment in order to become aware of your limited perspectives and experiences. Change is to be embraced because of this reason – it should be celebrated. Experiencing other viewpoints can be a liberating experience, one that can ignite passions not yet realized.

Babette's Feast shows us how joy and new experiences get crushed when living in a contained community. The film is set in nineteenth century Denmark, in a small and isolated village. There's not much variety in the lives of two sisters until Babette, a famous Parisian chef, comes to live with them. She introduces the two sisters to her exquisite French cooking during a celebration for the 100th anniversary of their father's birth. At first, the dinner guests are hesitant because it's so outside the norms and traditions of their village. However, once they let go and enjoy the meal, you see a new passion ignite and their joy is apparent. Babette opens the entire community's mind to the joy of food and celebration.

When we cling to the rules, we lose our depth perception and our choices and outcomes become limited. It's passion that gives us our overall dimension, our depth perception. If you're always playing by a set of rules, you can't access passion. When you allow your passion to guide you, the rules don't matter so much anymore; the rules then become a guideline. It's passion that opens up diverse possibilities of emotions, and along with this, life experience.

How Do You Recognize When the Rules Are Squelching Your Passion?

When you notice that you're changing yourself to match a set of rules, ask yourself the question, "Who is setting these rules, and do they fit for me?" In the movie *The Invention of Lying*,[80] nobody is aware that they're living by a set of rules that everyone has bought into blindly.

Just like the individuals in this film, we all have a tendency to gravitate towards people that have similar beliefs and rules to ours, making it difficult to experience anything new. When Mark Bellison (Ricky Gervais) discovers lying, it's as if he has broken out of this type of unconsciousness. He's liberated from the rules, and he starts creating new ones.

This lack of diverse experience can become a source of sadness and depression, similar to what we see in the movie. Some of the characters are not sure why they're unhappy because they're playing by the rules. This is similar to how we approach our jobs: if we get the right degree and then the right job, if we work hard and play the game, we should win at the financial game.

When it doesn't happen, we aren't sure what to do. We find ourselves saying, "Why did this happen to me? I played by the rules, and I'm a good person." *The Invention of Lying* gives us an example of how rules become a distinct consciousness, a way of looking at the world, a way of discerning life that becomes difficult to become aware of because it just seems to be truth. As a result, this limiting consciousness holds us back from experiencing more. If you feel any of these symptoms, then perhaps your rules are squelching your passion.

We Cling to Past Pleasure

Our memories of past pleasure can also become a groove when we become addicted to experiencing them again. If we're not careful, we can become obsessed with trying to attain the pleasure again. We cling to a type of craving that squelches our passion. This can distort our guidance and keep us stuck. Detaching from pleasure allows you to have an inner freedom. If you realize it again, that's nice, but you're not stuck wallowing if you don't. Clinging to past pleasure and desires prevent you from living in this moment and holds you back.

We Get Stuck in Past Suffering

Our past trauma can create grooves that keep us stuck. We're so afraid of experiencing similar pain again that our aversion creates a deep groove. It blocks our passion and keeps us from experiencing new passions in our lives.

In the movie *The Ugly Truth*,[81] Mike Chadway's heart has been broken. To protect himself from heartbreak again, Mike (Gerard Butler) becomes cynical about relationships. His cynicism about men and women becomes a source of entertainment that leads him to a radio job and then becoming a TV personality. While his observations are often humorous, they push love and passion away from him. His fear of being hurt again keeps him from experiencing a new love. This groove becomes a barrier that keeps him from true heart-connections.

Clinging to past pain or suffering keeps you deep in your groove, unaware that new passions are waiting for you. Remember, once was enough; don't keep relieving the pain over and over again. When you can see these past two-by-four events as an opportunity to learn, you can discover how to move away from the pain.

What Happens When You Lose Your Passion?

Without passion, you lose your zeal for life and can only see one facet of yourself. We are all multifaceted individuals. When you lose your passion, you allow one facet of your life to dominate: fear, grief, anger, or even joy. We are like crystals with many facets. When these facets are expressed, they connect with others' facets. We respond to match the perspective that is put out by others – this is one way we match up with each other. Diversity means that we can have many facets. When we allow the diversity both within ourselves and in others, we have more opportunities to connect and learn from each other. (That's why we like movies – they provide more scopes and mirrors to reference within ourselves.)

When you realize that you've lost your passion, try finding something that ignites your fire again. Try looking within to discover facets you weren't aware of. Then open yourself to connect with others with similar facets. Yes Man[82] is an example of how you can rediscover your passion. It takes something outside the norm to get it back. Carl Allen (Jim Carrey) was stuck in his past suffering: his wife left him for another man. He shows us what it looks like when we're clinging to our past pain. In Carl's life, there is no joy – only grief because his wife divorced him. Carl needs something to get him out of this focus.

Carl dreams that he died, and this becomes a two-by-four event (or as his friend Nick says, "a freakin' mind grenade") that gets him to want something different in his life. Carl realizes that on his current trajectory, he would be dead and his friends wouldn't care that he was gone. This motivates him to pick up the Yes Man pamphlet – which is interesting, because he just received the flyer that day. It was all set up for him.

When Carl attends the Yes Man personal development seminar, the motivational speaker, Terrence Stamp, tells him, "You can't audit life, my friend... you're dead, Carl – you say no to life and you're not living." Terrence convinces Carl to say yes to everything. This becomes the first time in a long time that Carl gets some feeling. His emotions are starting to thaw.

Stay Open to All Possibilities

"Yes always leads to something good," Carl reads in the flyer. "Never avoid opportunities. They may come in any form." Saying yes is analogous to being open to all possibilities. Once you are able to be open, synchronicity kicks in. When Carl runs out of gas, he meets his future girlfriend, Allison (Zooey Deschanel). This would have never happened if he had not been open to dropping off a homeless guy he picks up. Allison is passionate about life and helps him to see a new way of living life. Carl is attracted to her and the way she lives.

When you're open to all possibilities, you have more opportunity to connect to new perspectives with others. Carl connects with Norm, his quirky boss, and ends up getting a promotion. Norm's quirkiness was similar to Carl's, but Carl just wasn't aware of it at first. He's not just sucking up to his boss; he really is a match for Norm's quirkiness. This side of him starts to open up and reveal itself in the bar scene. Now that he's allowing this quirkiness to be expressed, he's more of a match for Allison and her uniqueness. Their unique way of having fun and looking at life becomes a match. This synchronicity provides more opportunities to connect matching perspectives with others, and their synchronicities start to build on each other's.

Carl discovers his passion again and starts enjoying life. He takes guitar lessons, learns Korean, and learns how to fly. He volunteers at the food bank. He ends up giving out loans to whoever asks for one, and he starts a new way of business: micro loans. He saves a man from jumping off a ledge and takes random trips just for the fun of it. Carl is living life carefree and courageous. Allison likes this unpredictable side of Carl, and Carl like how spontaneous Allison is. As she says, "The world's a playground. You know that when you are a kid, but somewhere along the way everyone forgets it."

Terrence tells Carl that saying yes is meant just to get you started and then you start to live your life from your heart with passion. Saying yes to life is similar to faking it until it's a genuine feeling inside. If you don't know which way to go, try on new things like you do with clothes. Put them on and see how they fit and look. It's not a big deal or major commitment. If they don't fit, put them back and try something else. Do you get upset when a store doesn't have what you like? Normally you don't, and if you do, you just don't go back to that store again.

Heart-Directed Passion

To create heart-directed passion, the five vortexes of emotion have to be in balance and harmony. When you have all five in balance, it feels like being in the zone or in the flow – not just in one area of your life, but in all areas where you're passionate.

Your passions also need to be in balance with each other. Think of harmony as being in peace and cooperation. You have a passion for your job, for your spouse, and for your children. But what do you do when they are in conflict? That's usually a sign that there's not something big enough calling you. It's a clue that some discernment and clarification is required. Passion and emotions can get messy. We like to think we can logically work through it, but it just doesn't work that way. Start by looking at what you really value. Is one of the conflicting passions more important than the other? What are the key things calling you? It's similar to creating a life mission. You look at the different facets and create an overriding structure, or mission. The remaining details will then fall into place. Your intent and clarification of this mission will bring the sometimes messy details of your conflicting passions into a greater balance and harmony.

In the movie *Waltzing Anna*,[83] Dr. Charlie Keegan (Robert Capelli, Jr.) has lost his way. He becomes seduced by easy money as a geriatric doctor and ends up getting caught manipulating the insurance industry with fraudulent claims. The medical board sends him to work for six months at Shady Pines, a retirement home/assisted living center in upstate New York. At Shady Pines, Dr. Keegan has to report to JD Reno, a former used car salesman and now the director of the retirement home and hospital.

The unscrupulous JD Reno is only focused on making money by selling drugs on the black market. He isn't concerned about his patients' well-being and has them all drugged daily so he doesn't have to deal with them. This experience provides Dr. Keegan with the opportunity to slow down and connect with his patients. He starts to see their humanity and their need for respect and love. Simultaneously, he falls in love with Nurse Jill. She helps Dr. Keegan to see a different perspective within himself, and he remembers why he became a doctor in the first place. His heart opens to her and his patients, giving him a more balanced passion for his work. He takes this new awareness and decides to change his life, eventually becoming the director of Shady Pines. We see how his passion for work and his desire for love come into balance and harmony, giving his life a new type of heart-directed passion that's not limited to just making a quick profit.

In the movie *The Hurt Locker*,[84] Sergeant First Class William James (Jeremy Renner) becomes the team leader of a US Army Explosive Ordinance Disposal unit. James is personally responsible for disarming over 800 IEDs and has become a leading expert in this line of work. He's good at what he does, has saved many lives, and enjoys his work. It matches everything that he wants: the adrenalin rush, the need to be a hero, and the ability to do it his way.

Sergeant James gets an immediate response to his efforts, unlike when he goes home to his wife and child, where cleaning the gutters and going grocery shopping is no comparison. He has a desire to be with his family, but his passion is disarming bombs. There's no way for him to find balance and harmony in his passion for his work and his desire for a family. Without some desire for balance, Sergeant James's passion for war wins every time.

The Hurt Locker also shows how he harnesses his passion for disarming bombs like fire. He's in the zone, with all parts of him working in balance and harmony to produce the unpredictable result of disarming bombs. He stays balanced and centered, listening only to his instincts; he tunes out everything else, including his teammates, that interrupts his process. He experiences an inner peace and cooperation with himself while disarming a bomb. No part of him is clamoring for attention over any other part, and therefore he can be focused totally on what he is doing. He's truly in the zone of that container, with everything working in balance and harmony. We see this also with top athletes or performers.

Notice what happens when he focuses his passionate revenge when Beckam is killed. He takes himself and his teammates into dangerous places that aren't within their skill set. As a result, one of his teammates gets shot accidentally by Sergeant James. He opened himself up to unpredictable danger that neither he nor his team was equipped to respond to.

In the movie *The Waterboy*,[85] Bobby Boucher (Adam Sandler) is a college football team's waterboy who discovers how to channel his passions as a football player. Bobby becomes skilled as a linebacker, not realizing this was a strength he had to offer. He visualizes his opponents as making fun of him and then channels his emotions towards tackling them. He gets really good at this and helps turn a losing team into champions. Others see what he's doing and use the same skill to overcome their blocks. Even the coach pictures his former boss as a crying baby, and this inspires him to find the creative plays to win the game. When we channel our emotions in a passionate way that has a clear intent, while staying balanced and in harmony, we inspire others by the accomplishments in our lives as Bobby Boucher displays in this movie.

Some Journeys of Passion Take Longer Than Others

Sue-Anne has clients, both men and women, who are passionate in their rage. While this does not give them the right to dump on others, they do need to have a safety valve. It's our job to understand how to use our own safety valve. All emotions serve, and you can take as long or move as quickly as you choose. Neither is incorrect. Normally, however, Sue-Anne's clients don't get the outcomes they want in a quick fashion, because they tend to judge themselves and this just takes them further down the road in the wrong direction. Eventually, they see that rage and then judgment is a longer way to go. It's a valid choice; it just takes longer to get back to balance again.

One's choice of learning can seem to be going in the wrong direction. As you are reading this book, if you identify with this way of learning, you need to be aware that nothing is wrong with going down this road of passionate rage. Is it the faster road? No, it isn't. It's typically a longer journey, because once you have dipped down into heavier places, it takes you longer to get back to places of peace – unless you have a major breakthrough in the depths of that place or groove, not unlike Byron Katie or Eckhart Tolle. Each of them had reached a place of deep despair and then created a breakthrough from there. Their pain was so intense and deep that they created a fail-safe process to keep them from returning to that place again. Eckhart Tolle discovered the power of now, and Byron Katie discovered the system she now calls The Work. While this is a possible way to get your breakthrough, it can be a long and problematic way for many of us, because we have a tendency to get stuck and never make the courageous breakthroughs that Katie and Eckhart did.

It's Never Too Late to Discover and Follow Your Passion

The two-headed dragons in *Quest for Camelot*[86] had been fighting for years. They couldn't blow fire or fly, but as mentioned above, one day they figured it out and found their passion. Remember, regardless of the path you choose, it's never to late to embark on your journey of discovery. Sometimes following your passion gets messy and can feel like hitting speed bumps along the way. When you experience this, remember this three-step formula to follow your passions and as a way of life:

- Let go

- Allow

- Communicate from the heart

The Rocker[87] is a movie about Robert "Fish" Fishman (Rainn Wilson) a talented musician in his forties who realizes his dream of playing drums in a rock band. As the movie opens, Fish thinks his life will forever be a search for one boring job after another. When he needs a place to stay, he moves in with his sister and discovers that his nephew is in a band. When their drummer can no longer play with them, he gets his opportunity to rock again. Fish helps the band by filling in as its drummer and getting them their first gig. Events occur, and the band members suddenly find themselves on tour.

Fish achieves his dream and follows his passion, even though it doesn't look like he thought it would. He doesn't let the fact that he's forty and the other band members are teenagers keep him from enjoying his passion. It's never too late to embrace your life's passions. Notice that every time the characters in this film hit a speed bump, they let go, allow, and communicate from the heart.

❈ CHAPTER SUMMARY ❈

Passion, when directed with intent, can shape an amazing life experience. When you live your life this way, you become a beacon of light for others. Your passionate life acts like a rocket in the sky for others to notice. The joy you feel from living this way will surely inspire others to embark on their own journeys. Because of you, our world becomes a more interesting and thrilling place to be.

BELIEF STATEMENTS REPRESENTED IN THIS CHAPTER:

Energizing Beliefs

- ❖ I live with passion motivated by hope and love.

- ❖ My understanding of love deepens each day.

- ❖ When I'm confused about the behavior of my loved ones, I take it up with them directly and don't listen to hearsay from anyone.

- ❖ I feel a bonded love connection with my mate that is tender.

- ❖ It's safe to allow my sexual fantasies and energies to go where they may, and I remember that I'm always protected and given a chance to choose vs. unconsciously react.

- ❖ My true friends love me whether I have money or not.

- ❖ I'm among the very young at heart, and it's a great way to live.

- ❖ I'm mindful about the food I consume, and I appreciate everyone who contributed to it.

- ❖ I stop looking for answers and find peace in what is.

- ❖ It's good to know your neighbors and help others.

- ❖ I help myself and don't wait for anyone to do it for me.

- ❖ I remember I always have free will, no matter what anyone says.

- ❖ I make a promise to myself to be open to life's possibilities and opportunities as they come my way.

De-Energizing Beliefs

❖ I can make things perfect for myself, my spouse, and my family.

❖ I hate to be late.

❖ Men only want one thing.

❖ I feel guilty and ashamed for just thinking about my fantasies.

❖ If you're with me, shut up and follow directions.

❖ I'll do anything to make money; it's just a matter of how much.

❖ I'll use any manipulative tactics to insure I get the money that's coming to me.

❖ I'm reactive with my choices.

❖ My life doesn't seem to have any meaning.

❖ I don't seem to be able to find my passion.

❖ At this time in my life, I no longer have any choices.

❖ I can never start over because of my age.

❖ I'm afraid I'll never be happy again; I'll never have passion again.

❖ I pass up opportunities for love that might have been terrific.

❖ Force is always the best solution when dealing with people I don't like.

❖ I'm afraid of losing my faith if I look outside of my religion for answers to life's questions.

❖ I refuse to change.

❖ I take risks to prove I'm alive.

❖ I blindly buy into the rules.

❖ I have to play by the rules to be a good person.

❖ I cling to past pain and suffering.

❖ I put money above all concerns, including my well-being.

MUSIC SELECTIONS

Bach Concerto No. 2 in E Major for Violin and Orchestra, Adagio

"An Unexpected Rain," Melissa Etheridge

"With Love," Hilary Duff

"The Chokin' Kind," Joss Stone

Lascia chi'o pianga, Handel's *Rinaldo;* Almirena's *Aria*

ESSENTIAL OIL RECOMMENDATIONS

Live with Passion: Revives the zest for life and helps recover an optimistic attitude.

Coriander: Has soothing, calming properties. Coriander seeds were found in the ancient Egyptian tomb of Ramses II. This oil has been researched at Cairo University for its effects in lowering glucose and insulin levels and supporting pancreatic function.

Nutmeg: Comforts, soothes, and helps boost energy by balancing the nervous system.

Gathering: Helps gather emotional and spiritual energies in order to achieve greater unity of purpose.

Surrender: Helps maintain feelings of equilibrium and inner strength and calms the heart.

CHAPTER 7

Take Yourself Lightly and Fly

When you don't take yourself so seriously, you can move through change less painfully and more quickly. It's as though a buffer of air lifts you over the potholes (or grooves), similar to being in a hovercraft. Taking yourself lightly is about getting out of your grooves peacefully. It allows you to rise above any emotion and you will move more quickly through them.

The three keys to taking yourself lightly are: let go, allow, and communicate from the heart. When you can remember these three methods, you'll find yourself flowing and flying more often than not.

Taking Yourself Lightly Is an Inside Job

Taking yourself lightly applies to all emotions, including the emotions of responding. Think of the so-called "fluffy happy people" who have a tendency to get wrapped in the emotion of bliss or joy. They are trapped in a sense in the groove of joy or bliss and thus must stay there, making it more difficult to recognize when another response is more appropriate (or more real) for any given situation. Additionally, there's a risk that others may feel invalidated if they are not in bliss or joy too. Some people tell us that we have to always be happy. If people like this slip out of their fabricated bliss of joy, it's common for them to judge themselves. Instead, you want to lean toward the feather – this is the lightness. It's the feathers that allow birds to fly.

The movie *Fantastic Mr. Fox*[88] shows us the contrast of taking ourselves lightly or approaching our problems with a rigid heaviness. Mr. Fox refuses to give up his wild ways of stealing chickens, turkeys, cider, and anything else farmers Boggis, Bunce, and Bean have to offer. Even though the farmers take every precaution to protect their goods, Mr. Fox always finds a way to win the game. The farmers decide to get rid of him and the other animals so they'll never have to realize theft from Mr. Fox again.

The more the farmers push, the more clever Mr. Fox and his animal friends become. Each time the farmers disrupt the animal's homes, they pull together, adjust, and find ways to make the best of it. This infuriates the farmers; as they get angrier they become obsessed with winning at all costs. They lose sight of their original intent as farmers and react in ways that jeopardize their livelihood. Their new focus of killing Mr. Fox becomes an obsession, they get more deeply stuck in a groove, and they forget what it means to be a farmer. None of their actions phases Mr. Fox and his friends – they simply enjoy life, adapting as they go. They just want to have fun and play the game of being alive. This movie shows us that taking ourselves lightly leads to more options. It also illustrates how it looks like when we get stuck in a groove and how it affects our actions and perspective.

LET GO... Allow... Communicate from the Heart

There are many ways to let go. Below are three affirmations that work well for us:

❖ *"I am not at the mercy of my emotions – I can choose a different way."*

❖ *"I do everything well, and that includes when I screw up."*

❖ *"When I choose to let go, I allow a new lighter perspective to show itself."*

We all experience times when our current situation isn't pleasant and doesn't seem to be working any longer. This could be a job where there's no life balance, it could be a marriage dynamic, or it could be your current financial situation. If you recognize situations in your life that don't seem to be working anymore, remember that you have a choice – you can always choose something different. Find a new job, go to marriage counseling, or hire a financial planning coach. Whatever the situation, you can choose differently.

Changing situations can be difficult; it can take time, and often isn't possible immediately. You still have a choice, and that is to change your attitude. When life circumstances seem insurmountable, you still can choose an outlook that serves you and your current experience. Many times we forget that we have a choice, and thus we get stuck in the heaviness of what is occurring. Life becomes difficult, and we feel like Norm Peterson from *Cheers* when Woody asks him how it's going. Norm replies, "It's a dog-eat-dog world, Woody, and I'm wearing Milk Bone underwear."[89] It's funny, but that doesn't help the situation.

You Always Have a Choice

Whether you know it or not, you're always choosing. If you believe that your current situation is the only option and you can't see any other way, then it will have to play itself out. By staying in your current situation, you are unconsciously agreeing to it. It always comes down to two choices: change your attitude, or change your situation. There's really nothing in between.

In the movie *The Proposal*,[90] Margaret Tate (Sandra Bullock) is a demanding editor-in chief at a prosperous New York publishing firm. Her staff fears Margaret; she's mean and at times downright scary. Margaret only has one dimension in life: her job. She doesn't have a life outside of work, and she expects others to be the same.

Margaret is so focused on her job that she neglects to renew her work visa. Margaret's supervisors inform her that she's being deported back to Canada, and it looks like she'll no longer have a job. Margaret comes up with an idea that could keep her in the US: she pretends to be engaged to her assistant Andrew Paxton (Ryan Reynolds) to overcome the immigration predicament. While this is a clever solution, the only way it will work is for attitudes to change.

Andrew tries to resist Margaret's demand that he marry her, but she threatens his career and forces him to acquiesce. He's so afraid of Margaret that he's willing to risk going to jail to preserve his upward path at the firm. In varying degrees, Andrew is similar to most of us these days. We force ourselves to work incredibly hard because we're certain that, if we don't, we'll lose our dream of improving our lives through a better job, a higher salary, etc.

Both Margaret and Andrew have made work their life. They like what they do, but they may not be able to continue working together because of the current circumstances they face. In order to prove they are really a couple, Margaret returns with Andrew to his home in Alaska. Grandma Annie (Betty White) is turning ninety and the family is having a big party.

As Margaret and Andrew act as a couple, they begin to change their attitudes. Margaret starts to see Andrew as a person and not a thing. She gets to know him and discovers new attributes and characteristics about him. Her attitude changes, she becomes softer, and she starts to enjoy his company.

Andrew stops seeing Margaret as such a horrible person. We get a sense of how he feels about her when Grandma Annie meets Margaret and asks, "Do you prefer Margaret or Satan's Mistress?"

Margaret and Andrew lighten their attitudes toward each other. A spark between them is ignited, and they fall in love. Now this marriage strategy doesn't seem like such a bad idea. Because both of them were able to change their attitudes, they are able to find a solution to their work circumstances.

When you revise your outlook and change your attitude, typically your situation improves too. An optimistic attitude is like a blessing or a prayer toward your current circumstances. See your attitude choices as sending blessings to your current situation. A good attitude can be a powerful prayer with a tangible effect.

We've all been in situations where there was nothing we could do. We get stuck in a traffic jam, our flight is delayed, or the weather changes our plans. We can find ourselves facing an illness, the loss of a job, or some other major change. No matter how difficult the circumstances, you can always change your attitude. If you don't, you'll just be miserable. It's the one resource you always have.

Life is continuously changing, and in our modern times the pace seems to be increasing. When you choose an optimistic attitude, change won't be as painful. You may even discover solutions that can assist you and others. Make it a daily practice to take your optimism vitamins each morning, and remember that you always have this choice.

Slow Your Life Down and Watch It Change

Most of us know how to drive ourselves, maximize our time, and continuously look for ways to create efficiencies. Being productive in every moment is our goal. What we don't realize is that the next jump in productivity is synchronicity. Synchronicity is defined as the experience of two or more events that are casually unrelated occurring together in a meaningful manner. To count as synchronicity, the events should be unlikely to occur together by chance. This is the ultimate way to energetically leverage yourself. You no longer have to make it happen. When you allow yourself to slow down, you discover new ways to be inspired by life, answers to problems appear, and opportunities for a better life are discovered.

In the movie *A Good Year*,[91] Max Skinner (Russell Crowe) is a British investment broker who inherits his Uncle Henry's (Albert Finney) chateau and vineyard in Provence. Max spent much of his childhood with his beloved uncle, and he has fond memories of their time together. Max discovers how to slow down, how to appreciate the beauty of life, good food, and wine, and he discovers companionship that blooms in its own way and timing.

As Max grieves the death of his uncle, a series of events at work result in him losing his job. It becomes difficult for him to be in both worlds. You can't be both fast and slow at the same time. Max's memories reveal the passion his uncle had for living. We hear these sentiments echoed from the resident winemaker as he describes his passion for his vines and for making wine.

When Max slows down, synchronicity starts to happen for him. The more he tries to control events, the more circumstances prevent him from succeeding. Notice the synchronistic events: running Fanny Chenal off the road, taking pictures to assist in selling the estate and falling into the drained pool, getting sacked from his investment firm.

Let Go of Beliefs about Others

Sometimes we're not aware of how seriously we take ourselves, our beliefs, and our lives. In the movie *Whatever Works,*[92] Boris Yelnikoff (Larry David) is a cynical, hopeless person. He doesn't see anything good about life or other people. He thinks everyone has an angle and nobody is inherently good. Everyone and all institutions are flawed and worthy of his sarcasm. He really thinks that his mind is superior to others and that he's the only one that sees the big picture. These beliefs act like a noose around his neck, and every time he expresses them he tightens the noose more and more until he can't take it anymore.

Melody St. Ann Celestine is on the other end of the continuum. She's optimistic about life, God, and others. She takes things at face value and sees the best in everyone. Melody moves in with Boris and starts to stir him, even though Boris thinks she's just a simpleton.

Boris keeps waking up in the middle of the night with panic attacks. First he's afraid he'll die someday, then he has night sweats as the noose gets tighter. Life is so serious for him. Melody is a nice contrast to his heaviness. For the most part, she's happy and enjoys life. She takes everything and everyone lightly, and eventually she rubs off on him. Her outlook charms him, and it catches him off guard.

She wants to have a relationship with him, but he comes up with all the reasons why it doesn't make sense. She follows her heart; he follows his head. Boris thinks he has a great mind, and he thinks she's stupid and lacks education. "Love, despite what they tell you, does not conquer all, nor does it usually last," he tells her. Melody replies, "Your bark is worse than your bite." He thinks he has an outstanding grasp of the human condition, although he really has a dim view of the human race.

If you're a perfectionist, you're always going to look for what is wrong in order to try and make it right. As a result, you can't find a way to take life lightly – to you, life is a problem that needs to be solved. Many of us take life as cynically and seriously like Boris. As a result, we miss the feathers of joy and love, and we miss opportunities to enjoy life.

The truth is, we rub off on each other. Boris and Melody marry, and Boris becomes happier, even though he still thinks being pessimistic is the intelligent way to live life.

Melody's mom takes life seriously too; she's very similar to Boris. She medicates herself with alcohol because her husband left her for her best friend Mandy. She has a breakdown, gets shingles, and turns to Jesus to heal her misery. Then she meets one of Boris' friends and completely lightens up: she shows her photography in a gallery, experiments with sex and multiple partners, and completely opens her mind.

In this movie, we observe the different perspectives of a variety of people and how they respond when they are uncomfortable with new ideas. We see how the consequences of our actions affect others. At a certain point, Boris can't take it anymore. He jumps out a window and meets his next love. Everything comes together, and the characters create a new community where each accepts each other's diverse views and lifestyles. As Boris says in the end, "Every chance at grace that you can get, go for it – whatever it takes."

We all tend to think that we're the only ones who see the whole picture. As Boris says, "Greatness isn't easy to live with, even for someone with normal intelligence." When the characters in this movie start taking life lightly, they start enjoying it and become completely new people in the process.

Let go of your pictures of how things and people – and even yourself – should be. Your roles and how you see them get in the way of connecting with others at a deeper level.

It's not about getting real with yourself and creating another story. If you're going to make up a story, make up an empowering one. Getting real with yourself tends to create a heavier story that keeps you from flying. You want a joyful and lighter story to be your focus. This is the art of reframing that Sue-Anne is able to do with her clients. She helps them discover the story that relaxes them − not the one that makes them feel stuck and rigid.

FOUNDATION OF EMOTIONAL UNDERSTANDING
REACTIVITY vs RESPONSE

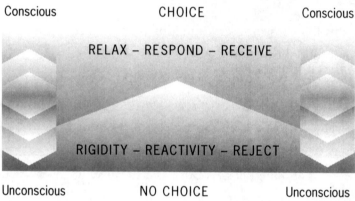

Conscious   CHOICE   Conscious

RELAX − RESPOND − RECEIVE

RIGIDITY − REACTIVITY − REJECT

Unconscious   NO CHOICE   Unconscious

When we put ourselves in a box of rigid belief systems, it keeps us from discovering other sides of ourselves. If we first recognize how we do this to ourselves, we're then able to see how we do it to others. These boxes can be political, social, religious, cultural, or some other construct.

How does this apply to your own relationships? Do you have constructs and beliefs about who you think your mate is or is not? Are you able to see all of his or her perspectives, or have you fallen into the trap of fixating only on a few? In *Whatever Works*, watch how Melody latches on to the perspective of Boris as a ballplayer and doesn't let it go.

It's possible that you really don't know your mate, and yet you're frustrated with how your relationship is playing out. The perspective you desire could be right there for you, but you just can't see it. On the other hand, perhaps it was never there and you merely thought it was. We tend to think that putting others in a box will give us some predictability about who they are and how they will respond. We're afraid that if we don't keep them in this box, they'll become unpredictable. We'd rather deal with the known than have to deal with change. Even though the unknown could turn out to be a surprise and delight, we won't let ourselves explore the possibility.

Attitudes and Beliefs Can Become Limiting Boxes

When we're rigid we get reactive; when we relax we have more opportunities to respond to what is going on in our life. Rigidity leads to reactivity and rejection of anything new. Relaxation leads to responding and discovering the rewards that come from this place of choice.

Give Up Your Addiction to Pleasing

Stay focused on your own emotions and what's happening in your own life. If you don't, you can easily be sucked into another person's groove. Stay out of the need to fix things for others. It's just another form of pleasing that doesn't serve you or the one you're intending to help. You can be there for loving and centered support, but there's no reason to join them in their groove.

Wait Your Hurry

When Sue-Anne's beloved grandmother would notice her trying to move too fast and getting flustered, she'd remind Sue-

Anne, "Wait your hurry." It's a clever phrase that reminds us to put our hurry tendencies on hold or on pause. When we're always in a hurry, we're usually trying to force something to happen. It's as if we can manufacture a spark of creativity or magic by pushing upstream, but that's not actually how it usually happens. Creativity is a process where you let go and see where the stream takes you.

When asked about his creative process, Jimmy Page, lead guitarist from Led Zeppelin, said, "I can't tell you what the process is. It changes from one thing to another. But it usually comes for anybody who's writing, whether it's the written word or music or whatever. It just comes from the creative spark... it's all very spontaneous. But you see the whole reason for being here was for that."[93]

Deepen Your Ability to Discern What Is Going On

In a particular situation, see if you feel pulled or pushed. If you feel like you're being drawn to something and you have all sorts of logical reasons why you shouldn't do it, yet it brings a smile to your face or a warmth to you body, then you know you're being led, being pulled, toward it. If you feel like you have to really push yourself and feel totally pressured, it's an indicator that it's not the right thing. There have been times when Sue-Anne has been led to purchase a sacred statue or some other item that she's drawn to. She knows she's being pulled or encouraged to buy whatever is before her, even though rationally it might not make financial sense. She's learned not to resist these feelings and just go with it.

You don't have to push yourself through your weaknesses. If you use this principle in all areas of your life, you'll find you can get much more accomplished, but in a lighter way, because you're operating with your heart and body wisdom instead of your rational mind.

Let Go of Doubt and Have Faith in Yourself

Believe something so strongly that no other thought can get in. Believe that things are getting better without any doubt. The more you believe in yourself with unquestionable faith, the lighter you will feel.

Mind Your Own Business and No One Else's

What you do is no one else's business, and if you believe that, you in turn have to do the same for others. Mind your own business and no one else's. When we mind other people's business, we're keeping score. After we've tallied the score, we then feel compelled to spend more energy gossiping about the news. Gossip is another way we drain our energy, and it becomes a habit if we're not aware. It drains our energy, blocks our inherent goodness, and rarely allows us to feel good about ourselves.

As Jim Carrey tweeted, "Watching and reading gossip is like eating somethin' greasy. Fun at first but afterward u feel gross. It seems 2 drain your vitality" (April 19, 2010).

Comparing yourself to others is another way you are not minding your own business. Comparison will take you off the path to peace every time. It bogs you down in ways you can't see. When you let go of the habits of gossiping and comparing, you'll always feel lighter.

Forgive Yourself

Forgiveness – whether it's directed toward yourself or others – relieves your heaviness. You might think that forgiveness is for the other person, but in fact it's always for yourself.

In the movie *The Mission*,[94] Rodrigo Mendoza (Robert De Niro) leaves his life as a South American native slave trader to become a Jesuit priest and student to Father Gabriel (Jeremy Irons). Rodrigo has to forgive himself before he can proceed with his Jesuit education, and Father Gabriel helps him to heal his past.

Once Rodrigo becomes a priest, the mission of native people is threatened because of political disagreements between the Vatican, Spain, and Portugal. Rodrigo quickly slips into his past groove as a warrior, putting aside the lessons of love and peace that Father Gabriel taught him. This movie, based on actual events, won several awards and is a moving story of forgiveness. It's an example of the countless leaders who stand for love even when it goes against the rules. As Father Gabriel says, "If might is right, then love has no place in the world."

Let Go... ALLOW... Communicate from the Heart

Allow yourself to be led. You might think that things will always be the same and that relief will never come. However, that's because the only frame of reference you have is the way things have always been. This is where you have to be willing to go into the place of the unknown. But you can't get there if you don't allow yourself to discover a new path. When you allow yourself to be led, you'll relax a little, you'll notice that others will come to assist you, you won't have to figure everything out, and you'll get guidance from many different places. Relying on your mind to figure out the solution limits your options and usually deepens the pain. Remember, your mind's options are limited to your current life experience.

Live in the Moment

Don't allow mental constructs to weigh you down. We spend so much time worrying about the future, thinking we know how it's going to be, that we miss what is right in front of us. We experience loss, health problems, death, and other life changes, and we wish we could go back to those moments when we weren't dealing with these challenges. There's joy to be discovered *now*. You have to believe that happiness is possible in the moment, or you'll keep settling for the set point of happiness you had in the past, focusing backwards, not realizing that there's a new set point that can be achieved. Otherwise, you'll just get more of the same with a few minor details adjusted. Same pattern, different story – the underlying song will still be the same.

Don't Dam Up Your Emotional River

Be like water flowing over and around the rocks (people, obstacles, etc) in your life. When you focus on the rocks, you build an emotional dam, and then it takes a wrecking ball to bring it down. When you flow around and over the boulders, they eventually become smooth. Nature shows us how much more beautiful a river is that has been allowed to flow over time; it builds the most beautiful canyons. These are far more exquisite than any manmade structures forced into a mountain using dynamite. Allow time to create this beauty in your life.

See Your Emotions as the Weather

Our emotions are analogous to the weather. For the most part, they're unpredictable, they occur for complex reasons, and rarely do they stay the same. Just like the weather, our emotions come in storms or gentle rains. Some days are sunny and balmy, while others are hot and steamy. Rainstorms come in all different shapes and sizes. We rarely fuss about it, knowing it's just the way it is. As the saying goes, "If you don't like the weather, wait a minute and it will change." The seasonality of the weather can make life pleasurable, depending on your outlook. Some rail against the weather and complain about its affect on them. Others love a good snowstorm or rainstorm – they enjoy the seasons and the ever-changing process of nature.

When you can see your emotions like the weather, they too can be pleasurable. It just depends on your outlook. As much as you'd like to control your emotions, it's like trying to control the weather. Let go of the need to control your emotions and allow them to express themselves The more you practice this outlook, the more quickly you'll move into joy and peace of mind.

Don't Take Anything Personally – Just Be Curious

Notice when you take something personally – it means that you're judging yourself or someone else. Instead, just be curious about what is happening. Be curious about what another person says or does. Be curious about why you feel the way you do. The more you can be curious, the less you will judge, and the more you will reach for understanding instead of standing in one place, intensifying your feelings.

If You're in a Fog and Not Sure What to Do Next...

When you're in heaviness, you're in a fog. You can't make sense of anything, and it's easy to get upset with yourself and others around you. You can't see the shore, the sun, or anything else. If you recognize this feeling, remember that when you're in a fog, taking action or moving in a certain direction won't help. So how can you have clarity when you're in a fog? You can't – you have to wait for the sun to come or light from another source. You have to be at peace with not being able to recognize the way. If you're the type of person that has to achieve, do something that doesn't require forward action. Clean out your closets, work in the yard; find a way to slow down and wait. Clarity will return when the fog lifts – and the fog *always* lifts. Hold on and things will most definitely change. When you're in the fog, slow down; you can't see the path ahead. If you were driving a car, isn't that what you would do? If you don't slow down, you'll be tortured by your mind about what might be in front of you that could cause harm.

Be Lighter with Each Other

The two-headed dragons in *Quest for Camelot*[95] had to get lighter about their unique approaches. One was fussy and snarly, and the other was fluffy – wanting everything to just be nice. The two had to become peaceful with each other's approach. Each dragon had to take itself lightly, along with its partner, and then they could fly, even though their wings were tiny. These dragons help us to see that when we trust others with differing viewpoints than our own, we see that both have value and are necessary. Usually the outcome is better too. Remember, we all want the same things in life: the desire to survive, the desire not to suffer, the desire to be free, and the desire to live in Utopia.

In Disney's movie *Enchanted*,[96] Giselle (Amy Adams) is a fairy-tale princess sent to earth by the evil Queen Narissa. Giselle left her cartoon fairy-tale existence and landed in the harsh world of New York City. She had never experienced the range of human emotions – what it's like to be cold or how pouring rain feels on her skin. Giselle is fascinated with this world of feeling, and her childlike approach attracts everyone she meets. In her cartoon world, everything always worked for her. Life is filled with joy and possibility. Love is romantic, to be celebrated with song and dance.

Giselle meets Robert Phillip (Patrick Dempsey), and he becomes her guide to the reality of life in this new world. Robert's first marriage experience hurt him in a way that he still carries with him. To keep from being hurt again, life has become practical and rational for him. Living is a serious endeavor, and he's resigned to see life through these glasses in everything he does. In his world, there's no room for playful expression, and magic doesn't exist. He tries to pass on these beliefs to his young daughter, Morgan, but she's skeptical and doesn't buy into his perspective. Robert is trying to protect his daughter because he doesn't want her to feel the pain that he has felt. As Robert explains to Giselle, "I just want her to be strong, you know? To be able to face the world for what it is. That's why I don't encourage the fairy tales. I don't want to set her up to believe that dreams come true."

Giselle doesn't see it that way, and she tells him, "But dreams *do* come true. And maybe something wonderful will happen." Giselle becomes Robert's guide to lightening up and not taking everything so seriously. Just like Morgan, she refuses to accept Robert's belief that life has to always be practical.

Robert observes the affect Giselle has on people wherever she goes. In Central Park, she dances and sings with others. When Giselle comes in contact with one of Robert's clients who is planning to get a divorce, she helps the client recall the spark of initial love. His client calls off the divorce and gives love another try. Robert is amazed at how others respond to her, saying, "It's like you escaped from a Hallmark card or something!"

Eventually Giselle rubs off on Robert. He starts sending his fiancée flowers, with the help of Giselle's doves. He buys tickets to the King's Ball and even goes in full costume, revealing his playful side. He allows himself to dance at the ball, realizing that life the way Giselle sees it is lighter and more fun. It's at the ball that he recognizes the spark and magic of love again. His true love's kiss happened to be Giselle's after all.

Notice that when Robert allowed himself to take himself lightly, he was able to find a love that was open and expansive. Before he was planning to settle for a love that was more practical to him, and romance wasn't a priority. We see that Robert's fiancée, Nancy, appears to be settling too.

Don't we all want life to be more joyful as it plays out in *Enchanted?* Look for those people in your life that are lighter than you and spend time with them. What makes them so joyful? How do they approach life? The more time you spend around individuals that have a lighter perspective, the more they're bound to rub off on you. If anything, you'll get some new ideas to try in your own life.

"Hey! Why don't we just say we have ninety-one percent full employment?"

Darwinism and Evolution

Recent studies suggest that all species are able to adapt if given ample time. When major change happens too quickly, some species can't adapt and become extinct.[97] People in your life have various levels of adaptability. When you can recognize their unique speed of change, you'll have more harmony within and without. When you allow people to adjust in their own way, with their own process and timing, you are able to connect with people easier, which makes you lighter and easier to be around.

Be Okay with Your Own Process

Everyone has a unique way of living life. When we can first accept our own process, we are then able to do the same for others. In the Sundance Chanel's TV series *Iconoclasts*,[98] Dave Chappelle's process is that he needs people, while Maya Angelou prefers being alone. You think you have to follow a process that works for others, but you have to find your own process and then follow it. Dave Chapelle also learned that connecting with his audience is where he discovered some of his best material. Be comfortable with making mistakes. Dave Chappelle says he's at his best as a comedian when he's not looking for a laugh. He had to get comfortable making mistakes in front of others.

When you recognize how you process creativity and emotions, be okay with them and let them do their own thing. Don't judge – just be at peace with the process and you'll be fine.

In the movie *Hereafter*,[99] George Lonegan, played by Matt Damon, has psychic gifts that allow him to talk to people that have died. He has helped many people with the grieving process, but George sees his gift as a curse because he thinks it means that he can't have a relationship. He believes he would always be able to see what would happen in the future and this would cause him much pain. He becomes obsessed with the belief that every relationship is cursed by his psychic abilities. His gift gives others relief, but it seems to only to give him pain. As a result, he takes a job in a factory and tries to shut down his intuitive abilities.

George attempts to be someone else – no longer a person that has psychic abilities. His brother Billy continues to encourage him to see his abilities as a gift that helps others. George continues to resist, but he can't seem to completely shut his psychic abilities off. People keep showing up in his life, asking for help.

George gets an opportunity to return to his gift when his company lays him off due to downsizing. Billy proposes a plan to support George as a full-time psychic. At the last minute, George changes his mind and goes off to London to find himself. He releases his resistance to being a psychic and starts to have some fun. When George completely lets go, synchronistic events present themselves and he ends up helping a young boy in London. The boy in turn helps George take a chance on connecting with a woman he met that day who's recent life experience dovetails with his own.

George Lonegan shows us that when you let go and stop resisting your process, magic can happen. He begins a journey of self-discovery while being okay with not having all the answers for what's around the corner. George gives himself the freedom to try something different, and each new experience leads him to another connection. In the end, George is led to the loving relationship he's always desired.

Allow People to Give to You

When you allow someone to give and you receive openly, you've actually given that person a gift, because we all feel better when we get to do something nice for someone we love. When you allow others to give, it's a double gift in a way – you get a gift, and the giver gets a gift.

Belief Is Power

Your belief is the pointer on your internal compass that gives you feedback on the direction you're headed. Look at your focus and what you are telling yourself, and you will begin to see the beliefs that are guiding you. The more you can actively focus on what you want for your life, the better. When you combine letting go, allowing, and focused belief, you have a winning formula.

In the movie *The Last Holiday*,[100] Georgia Byrd (Queen Latifah) is a dreamer that loves to believe in the possibilities for her life. She dreams of having her own restaurant someday and practices her recipes while watching Emeril Lagasse on TV. Each time she makes a dish, she takes a picture and puts it in a book she calls her *Book of Possibilities*. It's clear that Georgia is passionate about cooking – it brings her joy every time she makes another addition for her book. Georgia's *Book of Possibilities* also has pictures of the places she wants to visit in great detail, right down to which hotel she'd like to stay in. There are also pictures of her in a wedding dress with coworker Sean Williams (LL Cool J). They look like they've just been married and are headed off on their honeymoon.

While flirting with Sean, Georgia has a minor accident and bumps her head. After getting it checked out, the doctor informs Georgia that she has a rare neurological disorder called Lampington's Disease. Georgia discovers she can't afford the needed operation, and so she decides to liquidate her 401K and live the dreams she has always desired. She books a trip to her dream hotel for a ski trip in the Czech Republic. Once Georgia lets go, she starts to thoroughly enjoy herself. Her glowing presence and attitude inspire others. People enjoy her company and want to be around her. They actually think she's someone famous or important. Then magic starts to happen. Georgia learns that her diagnosis was a mistake, and her dreams start to fall into place. Her book is renamed *Book of Realities*.

Georgia's beliefs were so clear that all she needed to do was let go and allow them to come to her. Because of Georgia's outlook on life, she inspired others to follow their dreams too. This is a fun movie, and it's a great example of what can happen when you focus your beliefs, let go, and allow them to become realities.

Let Go... Allow... COMMUNICATE FROM THE HEART

When you speak from the heart, you are matter of fact about how you deliver your comments. It's usually from a place of confidence and a knowing that others are able to hear as your truth. Someone that communicates from the heart isn't trying to please others or look to them for approval.

You can view communication with others like peeling a hard-boiled egg. The egg is the person, the shell is their story, and it takes time to break the shell a part. Every person's way of cracking the egg is unique – no two are the same. Think of the grooves as the shell; you identify with it to the point that you think you're the shell, when in fact you're the egg inside. The egg is your true self.

We want our heart to lead because the heart makes all the emotions okay. They're all acceptable and they're all transient. This way we make everything that is going on okay and prevent the mind from judging us and invalidating these emotional states. This keeps things lighter and out of our emotional grooves.

When communicating, seek to understand other people and don't rely on your assumptions. Too often, we make assumptions about what people say; we don't slow down and ask clarifying questions, and this is the source of much of the communication breakdowns that are happening right now.

Our mind is convinced that its point of view is truth, and it will slice and edit what it's hearing in order to justify its belief systems. Clarity in your communications with others makes life lighter and easier. You can't reach peace by measuring from your definition of truth. Truth is always relative, and rigid rules are not. We might think that our doubt is truth — but we can see how doubt keeps us from peace of mind.

Be true to your own values, and you won't be co-opted from others for any reason. However, if you make someone larger than life, you won't believe that your way is acceptable. You won't give yourself room to grow and explore a new way of approaching life.

In the movie *Elegy*,[101] David Kepesh (Ben Kingley) falls in love with his student, Consuela Castillo (played by Penelope Cruz), who is thirty years younger than him. As his heart begins to open, he resists the feelings of love and the desire to bond with Consuela. He falls back on his old patterns of sexual possessiveness and becomes focused on being abandoned or hurt, which prevents him from enjoying Consuela in the present. He dwells how it might look for a man his age to be dating such a young woman. He'd rather be alone than allow himself to follow his heart and discover a new set point of happiness.

Consuela creates an ultimatum with David by insisting that he meet her family — her timing, not his. When he's not able to agree to this, she constructs a dam in the river that changes the direction of their relationship. She ends the relationship and tells David not to call her just when the relationship is at its most vulnerable. This is too big of a change too quickly for David. Everything in his world was structured and orderly, from his apartment, clothes, grooming, visits with his friend, etc. His routines are so deeply rooted that he requires time to learn new ones. This is not an unusual pattern for men. You can see that he values a set point that minimizes risk and is predictable. If Consuela could have flowed with him a bit longer, she could have determined more realistically if he was capable of coming around and bonding with her as she desired.

Be Real and Watch How People Respond

We all like people who are real with no pretense: Einstein, Willie Nelson, Oprah, Dr. Oz, and Dr. Phil. They're all authentic in the way they come across to us. We are drawn to these characters because we want to be real and loved too. Being real is becoming aware of your own foibles. As you know yourself and your foibles, you can create space between your reactions and responses. As a result, you're able to respond to that part of you that wants to unconsciously react. When you know yourself, you can create a pause that prevents the reactions, thus giving yourself time to choose your response.

We like people who are real because we don't have to guess who they are. We can relate to them because they show us emotions we recognize within ourselves, but somehow people still like them. As a culture, we praise people that react quickly. Ironically, we also punish quick reactions. No wonder people are confused. In corporate America as well as in politics, if someone isn't decisive and able to react quickly to any situation, somehow that person is not strong or not a good leader. However, the true sign of strength is actually the ability to know yourself; you can then pause and determine the best response.

In the movie *The Birdcage*,[102] we see a humorous example of what happens when you try to be someone you're not; everything is harder and things get messy. The more you fabricate who you are, the more you defer the messiness, and situations just escalate. Armand Goldman (Robin Williams) and Albert Goldman (Nathan Lane) are a gay couple that decide to fabricate their living situation to support their son and his future in-laws. They invite their son's fiancée and her conservative parents over for dinner. Armand and Albert go to great lengths to change the way they live so that Senator Keeley (Gene Hackman) and his family are comfortable with them. Their goal is to make a favorable impression for their son's sake, and in the process they try to be people they aren't. The two families experience a hilarious evening of mishaps. *The Birdcage* shows us that when we are who we really are, we no longer need to give any importance to what people think of us, whether it's favorable or not.

Ground Your Emotions

There are periods in our life where it feels like we're emotionally out of control. Our emotions seem to be running the show and we give others the responsibility for how they play out. We are at the mercy of our emotions – we become their victim. If you recognize this happening in your life, try grounding your emotions.

Being accountable for your own emotional reactivity is tricky business. What do you do when your emotions just seem to overwhelm you and you don't want to be reactive? You know that letting them flow is the best course of action, but that is scary because you are afraid you'll throw the emotion at someone. It all seems too difficult. This is your indicator that your emotions need to be grounded. This mobilized energy has to be released, and it is your job to release it. No one else can do it for you.

Think of your emotional state as a kite. Some of us have small, efficient kites, and others have large, ornate designs that fill the sky. Regardless of your particular kite and size, it must remain grounded. When a kite is not grounded on a string or tether, it can spin out of control. This can be dangerous to the kite. It's at the mercy of the unpredictability of the winds. There's no guessing where the kite might go: it could get stuck in a tree, continue to flail uncontrollably, or instantly drop to the ground. The kite can get damaged, or worse, completely destroyed.

When your emotions are not grounded, you open yourself up to unpredictable outcomes that can make your journey more difficult. So many of us want someone to hold our kite string for us and be responsible for it. Yes, there's a place for that support, but first you have to ground your own kite so others can then support you. The bigger the kite, the bigger the tether required to keep it flying while still anchored firmly to the earth. When you become untethered, you flail about, smacking those around you, taking them and you off course. When you ground your own emotional system, it's safe for others to support you.

An ungrounded emotional system can make you vulnerable to manipulation in ways you won't see coming. Your kite is now at the mercy of whatever manipulative winds surge past you. These influential winds come in many gusts and sizes. It can be a simple news report that angers or scares you. It can be your mate forgetting to pick up milk from the grocery store. It might be a passing comment of disapproval from a friend or loved one.

In the movie *Black Swan*,[103] Nina Sayers lands the coveted lead role in the ballet *Swan Lake*. Nina's deeply sensitive personality makes her a natural for the white swan role. It's the black swan character that intimidates her. The black swan's dark sides scare her. She believes that pushing herself to new levels will allow her to pull off this demanding role. In the process, Nina forgets her own strengths and doubts that she can pull it off. She puts an inordinate amount of pressure on herself and her body, and takes on the pressure exerted by her mother, the director, and competing ballerinas. Nina doesn't appear to be eating regularly, she's not resting, and she starts making reckless decisions. We begin to see how ungrounded her emotions are. Her body is stretched to its limits and she's not listening to it or honoring its needs. As a result, she loses perspective and clarity, and opens herself up to dangerous manipulations.

Often others who instinctively know that you're not grounded can push your buttons (consciously or unconsciously). Not only does this put your peace in their hands, but these types of manipulations can keep you distracted from your purpose, from accomplishing your goals, and can delay the dreams you have for your life.

When your emotions are not grounded, you lose perspective and it becomes difficult to discern choices that can have a major effect on your life. You miss opportunities and synchronistic events. It also opens you up to potentially harmful situations that you're not even aware of.

But isn't Nina a success in the end? Didn't she make it happen by pushing herself to a new level? Nina does end up being a success, but look at what it cost her. When we push ourselves to this heightened level, it can create such emotional reactivity that most of us end up missing the goal all together. We get distracted and our dreams slip away. We're so close, but our emotions get frayed and we get lost in the weeds. (Listen to Paul Simon's famous song, "Slip Slidin' Away" and you'll hear some examples of what can happen.)

Sometimes the drama of our untethered emotions creates a pattern we don't see. Because our swirling emotional system is in such flux, we feel justified in letting it flail in the wind – thinking we're at its mercy and there's nothing we can do. If you recognize these feelings, you're probably not staying grounded emotionally. Remember, the bigger the kite, the more grounding required. As we embrace being alive and remember our humanness, our emotional journey becomes a pleasurable adventure.

How Do You Ground Your Emotions?

Think of your emotions as mobilized energy that requires a lightening rod to ground it. A lightening rod provides a low-resistance path for the electricity to transfer into the ground. It takes the harmful current away from the structure and safely to the earth. When you find a practice that can become your emotional lightening rod, you and others will be protected from this intense energy. There are many ways to do this and we encourage you to find what works for you. Here are some suggestions that have worked for us:

Move Your Body Daily

Each of us has to find our own way to regularly move our body. For most of us, it's finding a daily practice that's flexible and adjusts to how we're feeling in the moment. For some, a daily walk is all that is needed. Others go to the gym, practice yoga, or do aerobics. Still others need a combination of physical activities along with a daily meditation practice.

Hugh Jackman says, "There are many things I do on a day-to-day basis... to prepare myself for the unexpected. I exercise everyday... mentally that puts me in a clearer place."[104] Depending on the size of your kite, you may need physical activity breaks throughout the day to help keep you grounded. When Sue-Anne is grounding her emotional energy, she cleans her house. She'll clean everything from the floors to a cupboard that needs to be organized.

Be in Nature

Find time regardless of the season to experience nature. Be outside around trees, flowers, birds – anyplace that's calm and beautiful. If you live near water, try walking near it as often as possible. Getting outside every day can keep us grounded and calm.

Have a Dedicated Daily Quiet Time

There are many ways you can create your own daily practice of quiet time. Some people meditate, while others pray, cook, read, etc. When you find your own practice, return to it daily and it will help you ground your emotions. "I meditate twice a day – it gives me a finer energy to be able to meet the world."[105]

Be Mindful of Your Food

Food can be a powerful source of grounding, especially if you're not currently mindful of what you're eating. There are countless resources that provide guidance in what foods are best for your system, support your health, and correspond with the seasonal changes. Dan Buettner wrote a book called *The Blue Zones*[106] after he discovered ways people throughout the world have mastered longevity. Many of the ideas in his book can help keep your emotional system grounded.

Get The Rest Needed for Your System

Many times we overlook the need for rest – especially in our western culture. We live in a fast-paced, multitasking environment, and there never seems to be enough time for sleep, rejuvenation, and vacations. When you keep your body rested, your emotional kite stays grounded.

Now that you've discovered ways to ground yourself emotionally each day, it's time to realize that you have the choice whether to use these tools or not, even though sometimes your life might feel like you're in a rudderless ship with no ability to set your course or change it. It's when your emotions aren't grounded that you feel you have no say in how your life is lived. This can be a debilitating place to be, and if you're not aware of it, you can get stuck here and not even know it. It takes focused discernment to recognize this pattern in your life and to daily remember that you *are* in charge of your life and you always have choices.

Act as if All Is Well

When you live your life as though all is well, you live with an attitude and expectancy that always works out for you, and all your life experiences serve you.

We're not saying, "Fake it until you make it." We're talking about staying focused on your intent, knowing all is well. Faking it feels awkward, and it's not real for you or anyone else. How do you know all is well? You've already done the letting go, the allowing, and the communicating from the heart. This makes acting as if all is well believable, and others will sense your genuine confidence. This feeling becomes the lightness that gives you the wind to soar. This lightness gives you the momentum that prevents anyone from throwing darts or arrows at your vision. They simply bounce off of you, and you end up taking nothing personally.

In the movie *Dave*,[107] Dave Kovic (Kevin Kline) is the owner of a temp agency that helps people find work. On the side, he impersonates Bill Mitchell, the president of the United States, for car dealers, grand openings, etc. He's so good at it that he sometimes steps in for the real President Mitchell. When the president has a debilitating stroke, Dave Kovic acts as if he is the president for a few weeks and thoroughly enjoys the experience. Even as things fall apart, he checks in with his core values to see what works for him and moves forward, acting as if all is well. Regardless of the power plays that come his way from President Mitchell's chief of staff, Dave continues to do his job without any doubt, fear, or excitement.

The Mind Can Terrorize You if Let It Run Wild

When your mind is in the driver's seat, it makes it nearly impossible for you to communicate from the heart. What you do with this fickle mind? You find ways to distract, motivate, and inspire it.

There's a story from the *Mahabharata* in which Karan describes the negative and fickle nature of the mind:

Karan was revered by everyone for his kindness and his great generosity. One day, he was rubbing oil on his hair as he was preparing for his bath. At that moment Lord Krishna arrived and asked for the jeweled oil cup as a gift. Krishna was testing Karan, for it was reputed that Karan would, without exception, immediately give away whatever was asked of him. He never postponed a chance to give. When Krishna asked for the jeweled cup that Karan was using, Karan was a bit surprised. He said, "Ah, my Lord, how strange that you should want such a paltry thing. Yet who am I to judge? Here, take it." Because Karan's right hand was full of oil, he placed the cup in Krishna's hand with his left hand. But Lord Krishna scolded Karan for offering with his left hand. (In India, one would never offer anything with the left hand as it is considered to be improper).

"Forgive me, Lord!" said Karan. "As you can see, my right hand is covered with oil, and I was afraid that during the time it would take to wash my hand, my untrustworthy mind might change its course and no longer want to give you the cup. My fickle mind would then deprive me of the good fortune obtained by Providence to offer you something. This was why I acted at that very moment."[108]

This is not the time to let the mind lead. If you're trying to make yourself do something and it increases your sense of torture, don't do it. Just relax, and you'll know when to return to whatever issue is causing distress.

Drama Keeps the Mind Spinning

Drama feeds the mind and keeps it spinning. It's challenging to communicate from the heart when you're immersed in drama. Drama has a tendency to spark our mind's reactivity. In drama you're unable to discern what your heart wants because the mind is off doing its thing.

Disconnecting yourself from others' drama allows you to fly, and this actually helps your loved ones by staying out of it. You can't join their drama enough to help them move through it. Be mindful of who in your life has drama patterns and observe how you react to them. Take a look at what you watch on TV. Some drama is entertaining, while other drama just sucks you in. Think of the way news is delivered – not just the facts, but with dramatic and sometimes personal editorial content. These types of news outlets are positioning their news to illicit an emotional reaction, which helps to keep you engaged and elevates their ratings. This is simply the business model that works for them, but make sure you're aware of what you choose to focus on and how it affects you.

Look for the Good in Every Moment

Another way to divert your mind when it's tormenting you is to look for the good in every moment. This helps you to feel true appreciation for everything that is going on. Practice this daily and notice how much lighter you feel. Don't expect yourself to always be in bliss. Looking for the good can help you discover hope or centeredness in any moment. All beliefs are habits of thinking. The more you practice the better you feel.

Another way you can discover the good is to create your own celebration practice. This is a daily habit of looking for the surprise and delights throughout your day. At the end, you'll have several examples of ways your day delighted you. It can be as simple as a phone call with a friend, or a delicious lunch. Before going to sleep, write down at least three things that either surprised you or delighted you. This is a good way to end the day and prepare you for a pleasant sleep.

God's List

Get clear on what's on your list and what belongs on God's list. If you can't figure out how to solve any issue in your life, put it on God's list. If you're supposed to be doing something, you'll feel the inspiration to take action. If you don't know how, it most likely needs to be on God's list. The Universe is waiting to be asked, so take the time to literally create a list. Write down all the issues that you just can't see how to resolve or that keep you from inner peace. When you find yourself worrying about any issue already on the list, remember to tell yourself, "This is God's list, not mine." Let go, allow, and communicate your desires from the heart – then watch the divine unfold in your life!

❈ CHAPTER SUMMARY ❈

"Whatever happens to me seems to happen for the best"
— Frank Capra

We all want to live a joyful life that feels light and inspiring. When you can let go, allow, and communicate from the heart, life becomes less serious. Find ways to honor your own process in ways that serve you. As Winston Churchill was famous for saying, "KBO (Keep Buggering On) is the order of the day." Churchill inspired a nation and the world by using this mantra for himself. It was his way of keeping his focus lighter, and in turn it helped those around him to do the same. When you can keep yourself lighter, you'll inspire others to do the same.

BELIEF STATEMENTS REPRESENTED IN THIS CHAPTER:

Energizing Beliefs

❖ I no longer feel the need to prove myself through competition.

❖ I'm getting better and better at recognizing who I am.

❖ Help is all around me, waiting for me to ask for assistance.

❖ My emotions are the most perfect guides, and I follow them, knowing I'm on the right track.

❖ My life doesn't sadden me anymore, and I love remembering why I'm alive and the possibilities of my dreams.

❖ I stay open-minded to meeting all types of people.

❖ I look forward to waking up every morning and enjoying another day.

❖ I accept the fact that I don't know what I don't know.

❖ I don't have all the answers on death, God, and the afterlife.

❖ I embrace my beauty as I am.

❖ I remember to daily ground my emotions.

❖ I see what I have in common with others.

❖ When I can't change my situation, I change my attitude.

❖ There are many different ways to live a joyful life.

❖ I act as if all is well, and everything works out for me.

❖ I focus on what's working.

❖ I forgive myself.

❖ I go for my dreams and leave my doubts behind.

❖ I lighten up and fly with ease.

De-Energizing Beliefs

❖ Winning isn't everything — it's the only thing.

❖ I think love is a beautiful mate that completes me and is the person of my dreams.

❖ I could never live without my technology.

❖ I don't do weekends and holidays — I make money.

❖ I can't enjoy my passion; I have to keep it locked away.

❖ My depressed feelings and doubtful thoughts about my life are who I am.

❖ I'm serious and practical because that's what works.

❖ I hate it when people don't take life and reality seriously.

❖ If I could just take a pill, all my pain would disappear.

❖ I resist learning new things and new ways to live.

❖ I'm afraid I'll be abandoned by my mate and will end up lonely.

❖ I listen to the wrong people and it prevents me from hearing what my heart is saying.

❖ I can't get over my struggles and pains in life.

❖ If my loved ones don't do as I desire, I use ultimatums to regain my control.

❖ I overreact to my partner's shenanigans.

❖ I don't listen to my body's pain.

❖ If I control every detail, then I'll be perfect.

❖ I'm addicted to my emotional tumult.

❖ I have no patience for myself.

❖ I need drugs and alcohol to relax me.

❖ I need love to break my spell.

❖ I don't know when to rest and think I can keep pushing myself.

❖ Might is right because it has always won in the past.

MUSIC SELECTIONS

"Wrap Me Up," Sagi Rei

"Away Down the River," Alison Krauss

"Taking You Home," Don Henley

"Sometimes You Can't Make It on Your Own," U2

"Ain't Nobody's Business if I Do," Willie Nelson and Wynton Marsalis

ESSENTIAL OIL RECOMMENDATIONS

Frankincense: Considered the holy anointing oil in the Middle East, where it has been used in religious ceremonies for thousands of years. It was well known during the time of Jesus for its anointing and healing powers and was one of the gifts given to Jesus at his birth. More recently, it has been used in European and American hospitals and is the subject of substantial research. It has a sweet, warm, balsamic aroma that is stimulating and elevating to the mind. Useful for improving one's spiritual connection.

Patchouli: A relaxant that clarifies thoughts, allowing the discarding of jealousies, obsessions, and insecurities. In Eastern cultures, it is commonly used around the house to provide general support for health and to help release emotions.

Ylang Ylang: Balances male and female energies. Attunes emotional energy, restoring confidence and peace. It has a sweet, soft, flowery fragrance that has made it a romantic favorite. Ylang ylang is extremely effective in calming and bringing about a sense of relaxation, and it may help with releasing feelings of anger, tension, and nervous irritability.

Clarity: Can be used to help restore mental alertness or wakefulness when you are experiencing fatigue or drowsiness. It increases energy when overly tired.

Hope: Helps you reconnect with feelings of strength and grounding, restoring hope for tomorrow. This unique blend brings together the benefits of essential oils with the power to uplift and balance the emotions, making you more open to the joys that lie ahead.

CHAPTER 8

All Roads Lead to Home

"All individual things pass away, strive on, untiringly"
— last words of the Sidartha Gautama, Buddha

When we say all roads lead to home, we mean that our life is about finding joy and happiness. Home is the place of joy, peace of mind, and your system being in balance. Home is the place of the heart, and the place where we learn. We believe that all roads lead to home, but some are more direct than others, and some are scenic detours. We take these routes for experience, so we can get the contrast that helps us decide what we want. Our emotions become signposts that let us know where we are in our journey and lead us on the way. When we reach for more joy, it creates another trip around the emotional circle of life. We have to be grateful for what we have and express empathy for the journey ahead – and then we have to let go of what we have and move into the unknown, which can generate fear. We might find ourselves getting angry because things are not happening fast enough.

This process leads us to discover an expanded joy, a deeper peace of mind. It's the reason we're willing to keep moving on the journey, and each time it gets better and better. When you start to realize it's a journey, you're able to recognize what works and also what doesn't bring the joy you once thought it would.

All emotions serve, and all paths lead home. In the past, the ancient Vedic teachers taught about neglecting or subduing the body so a person could realize spiritual peace. Liberation meant eliminating everything that is human. Then, through Sankhya philosophy that led to Buddhism and the works of Pantanjali, a focus emerged that emphasized detaching from the mind. As Christianity and other western religions flourished, spiritual practices became variations of the ancient past. All of these practices can lead to awareness and peace. Some can be heavier and take longer to realize, and there is some risk that you may get stuck. When you see all emotions as the lynchpin, you accept the body, the mind, and the spirit, which allows the emotions to be a new pathway to peace. This is not meant to negate any spiritual tradition or path; they are all sacred and to be respected. It's just a suggestion that there might be lighter paths to learning and spiritual awareness. Even Siddhartha Gautama (the Buddha) saw that extreme deprivation isn't the only way to go.[109] We can live as normal beings and still experience realization.

The Emotional Circle of Life five-star diagram from Chapter 3 shows the process of change, and sometimes you might get stuck in one of the vortexes that take longer. Don't get frustrated when you get stuck – just know you're moving through change and more joy is sure to come. Own where you are and acknowledge what you want to learn from each of the experiences. Getting frustrated doesn't help you move to the next stage; it just keeps you where you are longer. The reason for doing change work is more joy, more peace of mind. It's in this place of home that we experience the joy that we desire, the peace of mind of knowing we belong and all is well.

Take the wisdom of the elders and apply it to your journey. Both the older and younger generations' roads are different, but both serve. You may think you have to react against the previous generation so you don't allow yourself to integrate their journey, but the elders help us to see talents that we might miss within ourselves and won't acknowledge. They reflect our uniqueness back to us. Many times, we don't want to own our gifts, but the elders give us permission. Each generation learns from the other.

Comparison Is Exhausting and Slows You Down

Where you are on the path at this moment is not the same as where you were in the recent past, so comparing where you are doesn't provide the clarity you seek. You are continuously changing, and this requires you to recenter where you are on the path now.

Think of an athlete — a runner, a gymnast, a soccer player, etc. Where an athlete is as a teenager is never the same from one year to the next. Young athletes are constantly changing; their bodies are still developing and growing. Each time their body changes, an athlete has to adjust and recenter in order to keep his or her skills sharp. We are inclined to think that once we've found our center, it should be that way forever more, but that's unrealistic. Any professional athlete will tell you that this is an impossible goal. It's how fast you can get back to your center that enables you to get better and better at recognizing and readjusting. The Dalai Lama tells stories about fighting with his brother when he was growing up. Francis of Assisi is known for sometimes losing his cool but quickly turning it around. The more you go along on this journey, the more quickly you recognize when you're off center and learn to gently guide yourself back. Embrace your current journey, because when you start to compare, you invalidate your current experience.

Heart Wisdom

"When I do things that feel right, magic happens. I've done some amazing things, you know, and that's when I follow my heart. When I never follow my heart I always get it wrong." — Jamie Oliver, Food Revolution

See your head (or your mind) as being in the service of your heart. When the heart leads, it brings balance to the whole: body, mind, and soul. Ask yourself, "Is my heart running the show, or is my head?" This doesn't mean that the mind isn't important – it is; you can't negate it. Remember, though, the goal is an honoring of all parts of yourself. You want the heart's wisdom to guide you, and this shows through the emotions. It's about discovering the balance and returning more quickly each time. When you have heart wisdom in balance, all roads really do lead home.

As we've mentioned several times, our writing process wasn't what we thought it would be as we were working on this book. Ultimately, we had to let go and write from the heart, and then use our heads to get the flow and insure the content was organized.

When you follow your heart, things may not turn out like you think they will. Sometimes the timing isn't on your terms, nor does it look like you thought it would. When you follow your heart, you'll be led to situations that support not only your desires but others' desires too. Circumstances will come together to help you, and also solves the problems of others.

The heart isn't self-focused; it's where we connect to each other. When you're following your heart, it will most likely lead you to others. The heart is beyond thinking – beyond the ego. As a result, you don't have to figure it out. When you come from the heart, there's almost a built-in protection, provided you're allowing the mind's thoughts to go through the heart before you act.

When you use your mind to generate harmony with the world around you, where you live every day, this allows your heart to guide and connect you. Your heart then begins to lead you to experiences that you've always dreamed of, and you experience a joy that builds momentum within and with others.

How do you know when you are taking the path of the head through the heart? You feel lighter and joyful. There's an inner balanced feeling, a stability that's recognizable. When you feel heaviness in your heart and something doesn't seem in balance, this means there's something to take a look at; your head and your heart are not in agreement. It's not about making the head or the heart wrong. Remember to first calm your system with some of the suggestions made in Chapter 2: follow the breath, take a walk, listen to music, etc.

When you feel more centered, you're in a better place to discern what the heaviness is, or why some decision has you rattled.

Heart wisdom is a natural way of cleaning up your intent, and when it's in balance, it looks like passion, excitement, confidence, openness, and creativity. Others feel it – they're inspired by and drawn to those that live their lives with heart wisdom. It takes courage to live from this heart wisdom.

Charlie Bartlett[110] is a movie about a teenager who becomes the self-appointed school psychiatrist. He has a past record of getting kicked out of private schools and causing problems along the way. When he's sent to the local public high school, he finds a way to speak and lead from the heart. The movie shows how everything falls into place for Charlie when he lives from this place.

We might think that just because we started out life destitute, this is our fate for the remainder of our life. Or we might think that we have to fight against society to get what we want. The movie *The Blind Side*[111] shows us that all roads do lead home. Michael Oher is a homeless teenager who has little education and gets the opportunity to go to a private Christian school due to the intervention of a few people. Because of this school, he meets Leigh Anne Touhy (Sandra Bullock) who invites him to stay in her home when she learns he doesn't have anywhere to live. Neither Michael or Leigh Anne know where this is going to go; each just keeps taking the next step to see where it leads them. Leigh Anne and her family get the opportunity to look at things differently. They all begin to display the by-product of heart wisdom. You can sense that they all feel passionate about having Michael as a part of their lives, and others are inspired by their openness as well.

Our lives are filled with amazing technological advancements. As a result, we've become accustomed to having our days maximized surrounded by our modern conveniences. Perhaps that's one reason we don't take the time to look out for others or help those in need: it's inconvenient. We might have to change the predictability of our days and do something different. Or maybe our lives are so filled with work and activities that we don't take the time to slow down and see how we can make our community a better place to live. We hope that we can focus on that later in life when we're less busy and have more time and money. While it's true that helping someone takes time and can be inconvenient, the benefits usually outweigh the inconveniences.

Where do you start in your own community? "Smile... it lets them know you're their friend," as SJ says to Michael. Start small and see where it takes you. There is no better place to start than with your own family. When you can practice in your own home, you'll have more opportunity and skills to offer your community. This then becomes a practice that can show up in many areas of your life.

When people do nice things for others, we tend to label them heroes, which is a nice sentiment. But think about it — it's not the norm and that's why we see these individuals as inspiring heroes. Ideally, these acts of courage should become a normal way of being, not heroic accomplishments. When heroic acts are put on a pedestal, they become something larger than life to most of us. How do we live up to the standards of such heroes as Martin Luther King, Jr., or

Gandhi? Maya Angelou says, "Love is a condition so powerful that it may be the firmament that holds the stars... you have to have courage to love someone... without courage you can't practice any other virtue consistently."[112]

Think for Yourself

All roads are unique and individual, so find your own path. They only way you can do that is to think for yourself, not the way your group, family, marriage, politics, culture, or any other structured thought processes suggest you should think. We've lost this art. It's not taught in our schools, or in our homes. Instead, we're taught to pass standard aptitude tests like the TAKs in Texas schools. Our political parties tell us what side of an issue we should defend. We watch nonstop news and opinions to figure out what we should believe. As a result, we continue to get manipulated by half-truths with agendas that don't serve our own path. Perhaps it's a warped sense of loyalty that keeps us from thinking for ourselves.

We tend to take everything we see on TV or the Internet at face value. We assume that it's fact and not to be questioned. How is it that we have lost the skill of making up our own minds?

In the movie *A Good Woman*,[113] Mrs. Erlynne (Helen Hunt), an American from New York, is living in Italy. She meets Meg Windermere (Scarlett Johansson), another fellow American, in a dress shop and tells her during the course of their conversation, "If we're always guided by other people's thoughts, what's the point of having our own?" Mrs. Erlynne has just made a connection with Meg Windermere's new husband. It appears that impropriety is at hand, yet we don't have all the facts. This movie is a good example of what happens when we think our eyes and ears know what the truth is. Just because we see something and hear another doesn't mean it's the truth. Most of the time, it's just a slice of what is really going on.

A Good Woman shows how quickly we all can react to what we think is occurring without slowing down to determine what is really going on. We just get carried away with everyone else, not thinking for ourselves. In the movie, it all works out in the end, yet no one could have guessed how it would.

"Snobbery exists in all areas of life, not least literary criticism. By snobbery I mean any method of judging someone or something whereby you latch on to one or two features about them/it, and use these to come to a definitive, immovable judgment. In intellectual matters, the snob will often take the external features of a work as a guide to its value."[114]

How do you start thinking for yourself when information in our world is disseminated at lightning speed? Technology allows us to get news and information virtually anywhere twenty-four hours a day. To keep up requires an Olympic pace – Tweeting, Facebooking, emailing, texting, etc. How to deal with all this? First, don't immediately react to what you see and hear. Take time to allow your mind and thoughts find their way to your heart. It's in the heart where your emotions will guide you to what feels right to you. This is the place of heart knowing, or wisdom. Be willing to question any external information that doesn't provide that balanced sense of knowing.

Eat Pray Love[115] is a movie about one woman's journey of self-discovery and the steps she takes to learn how to think for herself. Liz Gilbert (Julia Roberts) tells us that she disappears into the person she loves, giving her mate everything until she completely forgets who she is. She begins to learn how to have a new relationship with herself by following her heart to see where it takes her. Her journey takes her to Italy for the pleasure of food and friends, then to India for prayer and meditation, and her journey ends by discovering love in Bali.

In each location, Liz learns to enjoy being on her own, celebrating life. She eats what she wants in Italy and doesn't feel guilty about it. In India, she discovers moments of peace that open her heart and prepare her to love again. By the time she gets to Bali, Liz is starting to enjoy herself, and there's a glow about her that's apparent to others. Even Ketut Liyer, the ninth-generation Balinese medicine man, doesn't recognize her. Two years prior, he predicted she'd return. When Liz reminds him of this prediction, Ketut still doesn't recognize her. Only when she shows him the drawing he gave her does he recall their initial meeting. Ketut tells her, "Last time you very sad-looking woman – now so happy, like different person." When they first met, Ketut told her that she needed to be grounded like the four legs in the picture and look through her heart rather than seeing the world through her head.

Liz shows us how she discovered being in the moment while being conscious of her feelings. Liz Gilbert has inspired many of us to look within to discovery our own journey. She gives us permission to explore life and find our own joy. Liz shows us how to overcome any of our self-imposed limitations when trying to discover our own path. What matters to *you* is the point – everyone's journey is unique and different.

Find Your Own Jet Stream

On the TV series *Iconoclast*, one episode features Archbishop Desmond Tutu and Sir Richard Branson.[116] We get to see how each man uniquely carved out their own version of a successful life. These extraordinary individuals have had a profound effect on the world and continue to inspire others to find their own path. Each was willing to seek a different way outside the acceptable norms. Both gentlemen think big and have the courage to pursue their dreams. When Archbishop Tutu asks Mr. Branson, "Why are you so successful?" he answers, "To fulfill your dreams... get involved with whatever interests you in life and do it the best you can." Branson goes on to say that he's felt extreme fear while on his journey. For example, on one of his transatlantic flights, he encountered complications that made completion of his trip questionable. The only way the passengers and crew would survive was for the plane to get into the jet stream and hope the speed would allow them to land in time.

When you set out to find your joy, find your own jet stream, face your fears, and expect the best outcome, you may not get exactly what you planned, but you'll be much better off than if you sat still and didn't take any action. Both Archbishop Tutu and Richard Branson remind us that when we think big, find our own path, and stay inspired, anything is possible.

Many of the great master teachers made breakthroughs in spiritual development when they were willing to challenge the conventional teachings of the day: Buddha with Vedic philosophy, Jesus with Hebrew teachings, and Moses with Egyptian rule by the Pharaohs as gods are just three examples. Because they were willing to get their answers from within, they all made huge leaps in human spiritual awareness.

Clinging to the comfortable norms of what has always been is not the place where breakthroughs, innovation, and creativity have been discovered. This is true whether you are talking about spiritual awareness, the formation of a business, art and music, or the resolution of the challenges that we all face.

Because our planet is so tangibly connected, your internal journey impacts all of us. Thinking from this place of the heart is where inspiration seeds the creative response that we all benefit from. It allows you to discover the unique facets within yourself that bring you joy and also make our planet a better place to live. It's here that all the answers to our current challenges can be discovered. Each of us has a unique gift to offer, a pearl to be revealed that could impact humanity in profound ways. How do you discover what that is, if you don't have the skill to think for yourself, to discover your own inspiration? It takes courage to embark on this road. This is an emotional journey that will lead you on your path if you just follow the emotional road map. On the way, you'll discover the unique purpose that brings you joy and fills you with peace of mind.

Don't Resist the Process of Life

All creation is a process. It doesn't matter if it's the birth of a child, the growth of a garden, or the creation of an apple. Nothing happens in the blink of an eye. The nature of creation is a process. See your life as a process that is working, and don't try to force that process.

You can't force an apple tree to speed up the creation of an apple. You have to wait until it's time to harvest.

Somehow, many of us fall into the pattern of thinking that life is a game that has to be won. If that's true, then life is full of winners and losers. If you don't play the game right and follow the rules, you'll be a loser. When you're so afraid this might happen to you, you push hard to insure you're a winner.

Alain de Botton suggests in his book *Status Anxiety* that our current meritocratic system indeed has evolved into one that has winners and losers. "In the harsher climate of opinion that prevailed in certain strata of meritocratic societies, it now became possible to argue that the social hierarchy rigorously reflected the qualities of those on every rung of the ladder, and that conditions already in place ensured that the worthy would succeed and the underserving flounder... a meritocratic system now added the insult of shame."[117]

In our meritocratic society, the belief is that if you have talent, energy, and skill, you should get to the top and win the game of life. Alain de Botton says that if you truly believe in this formula, then those that are at the bottom deserve their lot in life. He says, "Your position in life becomes not accidental but merited and deserved, and that makes failure much more crushing."[118] Anyone that doesn't rise to the top is then justly considered a loser.

If we truly buy into this meritocratic belief, we have to push ourselves to achieve ceaselessly until we make it happen. Alain suggests that making our jobs the great decider of our worth and true value in life is crazy. As a result, failure opens us up to significant ridicule and judgment. This insane belief system creates vast anxiety that is unnecessary. It keeps us running scared, willing to do whatever it takes to prevent a stagnating career – or worse, failure through loss of our job. If we don't find a way to "make it happen," we must not have tried hard enough. This type of thinking steals our peace and keeps us perpetually chasing our tails. It also prevents us from finding our own rhythm and flow in life. It causes us to live up to established norms that have nothing to do with our true path.

God Follows the Path of Least Resistance

The easiest way to see this is in nature. Nature always adjusts to its environment, be it the flow of the river or how a tree grows. The tree bends to the light; the river changes course, moving boulders and mountains along the way. The land regenerates after a hurricane or volcano; it always embraces the changes. All of creation follows this path and is happier for it.

You too want to follow a path that provides the least resistance to forward motion in your own life. By allowing this path, you have the most access to your own unique creativity. It doesn't matter what your walk in life is, we all need creativity as a resource. When you are on the path of least resistance, you are open, flowing, and not trying to make an outcome fit into a certain mold.

Sometimes it's easier to see how acclaimed artists, directors, and musicians do this. We have a tendency to discount the fact that we too have our own unique brilliance that is equally valuable, although it just may be undiscovered at this time. In a sense, we're all artists waiting for our outlet. This means that you honor your own talents and gifts.

In the movie *Sketches of Frank Gehry,*[119] the acclaimed architect, Frank Gehry, likens his creative process to following a ball of yarn that fell off a table. He explains that it's like a cat watching to see where the ball will go, staying curious and fascinated along the way.

In another episode of the TV series *Iconoclast*, Quentin Tarantino tells Fiona Apple: "...To me, the writing and dialogue is so easy, I actually feel a touch of fraud taking credit for it, even though I'm protective of it... it's like some sort of God antenna."[120]

Fiona Apple relates to his example of the creative process and responds, "And most of the time is spent just keeping the antenna out there, and that's 90 percent of the time... then all of sudden you go '... Okay, I'm full,' and you sit down and it goes." Fiona says that's when her creative process flows. When nothing is going on, neither artist worries about it, knowing inspiration will come back when it will.[121]

Your emotions will let you know if you're on the path of least resistance or not. When you are in the flow, it feels like excitement, fun, anticipation – everything seems easy. Compare this to being out of the flow, which manifests as anxiety, frustration, irritability, wanting to quit – everything feels extremely difficult. Feeling like you have to "make it happen" in any area of your life is usually an indication that you're not following the path of least resistance.

The concept of "making it happen" has become a success formula that is being taught globally as the way of attaining what you want in life. You work hard, you stay up late, you push yourself beyond your limits, pounding the square peg into the round hole no matter what. You don't wait for the right time, or some "God antenna" to pick up the direction; instead, you push on, never stopping until you've achieved your goal. This route requires a tremendous amount of energy, negates your emotional system, and can be challenging to maintain. Many of us follow this formula because it seems like the only way to be successful in life, and we think that if we don't it means that we don't deserve success.

Think about how a sailboat uses wind power versus an onboard engine. When a sailboat uses its sails to harness the wind, it is able to move much faster than by using an engine, and it's also a lot more fun. Following the path of least resistance doesn't require the same amount of energy as making it happen, and as a result, you can achieve much more simultaneously. As Quentin Tarantino says, "It's so easy." He's describing what inspiration feels like.

Making it happen, on the other hand, is trying to force inspiration, which is not possible. Making it happen is like trying to force the wind for a sail – it's simply not possible. This is not to say that you don't motivate yourself to take the next step in a new direction or complete a task that requires attention. Following the path of least resistance will help you discover inspiration, and this is where limitless creativity emerges. The more you follow the path of least resistance in your life, not only will you have more creative flow, but you'll also be able to sustain joy for longer periods of time.

In the movie *How to Train Your Dragon*,[122] Hiccup is a young boy who wants to fit in with the dragon slayers of his Viking village. He's very creative, and he uses these skills to develop new ways to stop the dragons. When one of his inventions takes down the most feared dragon, he gets a chance to kill it to prove his place in the village –

except he can't go through with it and ends up releasing the dragon, setting Hiccup on a journey of discovery that changes his and the entire village's perspectives on dragons.

Hiccup trusts his instincts when he's around his dragon, but they get distorted when he's around his dad and the other village leaders. Hiccup isn't as physically strong or as large as the others in the village, so he compensates by using his creativity. This becomes the road of least resistance for him, because he simply can't match the other dragon slayers physically. Once he gets close to the dragon, he recognizes that the vulnerability and fear in the dragon is similar to the way he feels, and this changes his thoughts about dragons. He's willing to question everything he thinks about dragons. Hiccup doesn't create a campaign in defense of dragons, nor does he start a protest against the dragon slayers. He doesn't push against their belief systems, deciding to keep his thoughts to himself. The more he learns about working with his dragon, the more he's able to work with the other dragons that are in dragon-training school. Hiccup's approach becomes one of gentle friendship, and the dragons are willing to go along with him. Eventually, his newly developed skill is needed to save his father and the other Vikings. He allows them to see what he's learned, and everyone benefits from his discovery.

Hiccup shows you that your own individual path is the one of least resistance for you. Not only will you benefit from following this path but your community will too, and who knows how big that could get? The right road for you isn't always the most elegant one. Too many of us are afraid to embark on our own personal journey unless we are assured it will end like a Disney movie. Many times, our road isn't the easiest one, and sometimes it can get messy.

In the movie *City Island*,[123] Vince Rizzo (Andy Garcia) dreams of becoming an actor but is afraid to let his wife and family know his heart's true desire. He is a corrections officer for the state of New York and takes acting lessons in the evening. His wife, Joyce (Julianna Margulies), thinks he's having an affair because of the consistency of his attendance at poker night, Vince's alibi for his acting class. Each member of his family thinks they're protecting each other by not telling the truth. Although it all works out in the end, we see how messy the journey can be when we resist what is and try to hide the truth. We also observe how resisting our heart's desire eventually is revealed; it just takes longer the longer we hesitate to follow our own unique path. We teach others by our example to do the same. When we're not willing to be truthful, others around us mirror this activity, we perpetuate the illusions, and we create more confusion for all involved.

Because Vince was afraid to tell Joyce the truth, it created a growing chasm between them. When we don't know what is going on, we make up stories and pictures to justify the missing pieces and then try to take action to calm our fears, without asking for clarification. This movie helps us see how it plays out.

Trust the Path

When we began writing this book and seeking to discern where our work was going, Sue-Anne turned to one of her wise mentors, Reverend Kay Hunter, for clarification and advice. Rev Kay (as everyone calls her) was enthusiastically supportive of our expressed journey, and told us, "It will be tough, kids, but it's doable." Neither one of us knew exactly what she meant, but those words echoed for the next three years as we followed the twists and turns of the road we've been on. If we had realized the journey would unfold the way it has, we probably wouldn't have embarked on it. As we came together, we each grew from this experience and created our own community. Coming together in this way allowed us each to heal in ways we didn't anticipate.

Our journeys together aren't always about us. We each have an impact on people in ways we may not see or anticipate. In the movie *As It Is in Heaven,*[124] Daniel Daréus is an internationally renowned conductor. His touring schedule is booked years in advance, and he is at the top of his industry. Daniel's passion in life is to open people's heart through music. Yet somehow over the years, he lost his passion and now feels there's something missing in his life. The constant touring is causing burnout, and it's starting to affect his health. Daniel decides to take a sabbatical to get some rest. He returns to his childhood village in Norrland, Sweden, to regroup and be alone.

Daniel's expectation for rest is revised when he accepts the offer to be cantor of the village choir. He rediscovers his love of music and bonds with his fellow musicians. The singers each have personal problems that affect their ability to sing together. But when they come together, their harmonies and song inspire them all, and they become their own community. They celebrate their wins and support each other through difficult circumstances. A type of healing occurs for all the members, and they're never the same. Through his connection with these quirky choir members, Daniel finds his heart again. It's as if he has found his own little slice of heaven. Daniel is inspired to write a song for one of the members and names it "Gabriella's Song." Daniel's song inspires us to find our own heaven by living our days as we desire, knowing we're good enough, and to embrace the happiness that comes with enjoying the gift of life.

Life is similar to learning how to ride a bike – it takes practice to stay balanced. Hopefully we have fun while learning to balance. Like riding a bike, life is easier when we allow others to show us how to get our own center, to find our own balance. We never truly know where our journey will take us or who we'll meet along the way. Usually, others help us heal in ways we don't expect, and this makes our journey so much more pleasurable.

The Wiz[125] is an updated version of the 1939 classic, The Wizard of Oz. The famous characters all desire to obtain abilities they are not aware that they already possess. They set out on the yellow brick road to receive these gifts from the Wiz, who lives in New York City. Along the way, they get opportunities to discover the abilities each one desires. The Scarecrow uses his brain to solve problems, the Tin Man discovers he's had a heart all along, the Lion realizes his courage has always been there, and Dorothy discovers the meaning of home. Each character has periods where they are immobilized and unable to embark on the road that lies ahead, but as their team comes together, they receive the encouragement from each other to continue going, helping each other to "ease on down the road."

Other people help us see what's really going on and how to discover our own unique abilities. Ultimately, each of us must decide to embark on our journey; nobody can do it for us. We may not like the obstacles we'll encounter, but it's these obstacles that help us discover facets, or strengths, about ourselves of which we were unaware. Once we discover these strengths, we can see how the obstacles served us and were actually a gift.

In the movie *Evan Almighty,* God, played by Morgan Freeman, says: "Let me ask you something. If someone prays for patience, do you think God gives them patience? Or does he give them the opportunity to be patient? If they pray for courage, does God give them courage, or does he give them opportunities to be courageous? If someone prayed for their family to be closer, do you think God zaps them with warm fuzzy feelings, or does he give them opportunities to love each other?"

Many times obstacles are taken care for us, as in the case with the two menacing witches in *The Wiz.* Dorothy and her team didn't intend to remove either; it was handled for them, and everyone benefited from the removal of these obstacles. Our journey isn't always just for us. The removal of obstacles generally serves more people than we ever imagined or intended. This makes taking the first step to ease on down the road more meaningful and inspiriting.

Remember, staying on the path while moving forward is your job. Nobody can do this for you. Notice what happens to the characters in *The Wiz* when they get off the path. They get distracted, and it just delays their trip until they can get back on the yellow brick road again. You have to be the one to motivate yourself to take each step until you can feel the wind of inspiration at your back. Additionally, don't get stuck looking for directions from outside yourself. The best guidance comes from within, and your emotional system will help you stay on the path that's perfect for you.

Course Corrections Will Happen Along the Way

Life roads aren't always perfectly linear. Our experience indicates they are more like a labyrinth. Just when you think you're far away from the goal, or center, in a labyrinth, you could be the closest to it. You just don't know it. Begin to see your journey as a labyrinth, not a from-point-a-to-point-b journey. You'll enjoy the adventure much more this way. Study the Chartres Cathedral labyrinth below and try to find the path that appears to be the farthest away yet is the shortest distance to the center.

Stop Judging Your Journey — You Can't Get It Wrong

Allow yourself to stop judging the path you've chosen. If you need to take a ten-year path, so be it. If you need to take a three-year path, it's fine. Remember that when you start judging the choices you make or how you feel about them, you begin heading down the other end of the continuum, keeping you from the joy and discovery you originally intended.

Sometimes what you're feeling along the journey is simply your body healing, releasing the old, and when you get on your case about it, you get sucked into the inner emotions on the Emotional Circle of Life diagram. The outer emotions help you move more quickly than the inner ones because the they allow you to respond instead of react.

While on your journey, you can be tired, not feeling well, and still remain hopeful. When you stop making a judgment about how you're feeling, it really is possible to shift to hope, and this helps you move back to your center or up the scale of emotions so much quicker.

Grace is a gift of God, and it comes from a higher place. The more detached you are, the more you allow the workings of the Universe, which means that you can allow grace, which is the gift of love from the universe. You go beyond "tit-for-tat" to a place that's above duality. Remember, love holds no grievances. Accept what is and be willing to grow. All that is required is a little willingness. Love must flow like a river; it is movement, not static. You can't be in love and fear at the same time. When you judge your journey, you essentially block this divine flow.

Seek Discernment over Judgment

Discernment (a response) means you have no value associated with something. It becomes perception in the absence of judgment (a reaction), which does have a value behind it. Look within and trust your emotions. These deeper emotions will give you increased clarity. When discerning, the first emotion is usually the accurate one, so follow it and don't let judgment trip you up.

Life Is Like BOSU

Have you ever been in a gym and noticed people training on devices that look like a blue half-ball? They do exercises on them while trying to stay balance. These are called BOSU balls. BOSU is an acronym for Both Sides Utilized. As the makers of BOSU balls say, "It's about inserting thought into movement. It's about asking our clients, fitness students, and athletes to be physically involved, but to also be *present* and fully engaged in the training process."[126]

Life is an ever-changing balancing act that requires constant recalibration. You only retain your balance by being in the moment. The moment you start thinking about something else, you lose your balance. Just like training on a BOSU ball, it takes focus and practice. The more you practice, the better you get at this balance. "I love the unknown... it's in the unknown that we live and breathe and move, all pretending it's the known.... If life can be a series of perpetual surprises, that's the most joyful experience you can have."[127]

Disconnecting from Others Is a Lonely Road

In the movie *Up in the Air,*[128] Ryan Bingham (George Clooney) stays as detached as possible while firing people from their jobs. Ryan flies around the country and lives out of his suitcase. Because he's rarely home, he loses touch with real, personal connections. Ryan gets a gentle wake-up call in the end, but it's unclear if he has actually decided to make the necessary changes to bring more enjoyment and connection into his life. At some point, this kind of routine detachment creates a numbing effect; we lose sight of people and then begin to think this is normal – the new real. Instead, the most important thing becomes erroneous goals like achieving the ten million mile mark, as it was for Ryan.

At the end of the movie, many of the people remark that it was their friends and family that pulled them through their terminations and other difficult life experiences. Since our families are so often removed, we try to create family in other ways. Many times we turn to our jobs for this connection, because there is no other place. We spend most of our time there, many of us move away from our immediate families in order to take a job, and then we begin to think that this is our home, our family. However, this level of connection is limited because of social norms and what's appropriate in the workplace. It might seem to work for a while, until the company efficaciously downsizes or terminates you – and then you feel like a family member who has died.

When we disconnect from others, we close down our heart. It takes too much energy to hold back the part of us that naturally wants to be open – like trying to keep the lid on a volcano. Most of the time, we're not aware that our hearts have become closed when we intentionally disconnect from others. Unknowingly, we become heartless, and we don't even remember how it happened.

When your heart is not involved in your interactions, it can look like you don't care – you appear careless. It can also look as if your actions are without thinking, or thoughtless. You're now on autopilot, completely unaware of how your actions affect others.

In the movie *The Caller*,[129] Jimmy Stevens (Frank Langella) is an executive in a multinational energy business who realizes that he has gotten lost along the way and has been involved in company decisions he now regrets. His mother tells him he's a shell of a person and doesn't need anyone. Jimmy is a French immigrant who found his American dream job after WWII. This consumes his life and who he used to be. He no longer has any traces of a French accent, and you'd never guess that he wasn't an American-born citizen. Jimmy's job requires him to be overly optimistic in forecasting so his company and other companies can thrive. Jimmy doesn't seem to have any connections to others and lives a solitary, disconnected life.

Disconnecting from others often seems to be the best way to protect ourselves from ever getting hurt again. We believe we have to disconnect from others to remain strong so we can have the endurance to make the tough calls, the hard decisions that our job requires. However, being vulnerable is a tremendous sign of strength, and it allows us access to our heart knowing, the instincts that help us stay centered, make better decisions, and find our way back to peace. An open heart is always a pathway to peace. Many of us are afraid to go down this path because we fear we'll lose control and will no longer be able to "make it happen" as we did in the past. Ironically, though, an open heart affords us more options that bring us peace and joy without gearing up to make things happen and staying in control. It's an interesting paradox.

Human Connection

We are all connected – this is not just some feel good aphorism. As Archbishop Desmund Tutu says, "You can't exist as a human being in isolation." He calls this *ubuntu*, "the essence of being human," and says that this speaks to our interconnectedness.[130] Journey's new lead singer, Arnel Pineda, the Filipino who was discovered on YouTube, and Susan Boyle of *American Idol* fame both experienced instant global success and acclaim. We decide what people, products, and companies thrive by the way we vote with our dollars, what we watch on TV, and how we respond to current events around the globe. More than ever, we are seeing the instant reaction to how we're connected.

All you need to recognize this truth is to remember how the whole planet went into a frenzy when the financial crisis started in 2007. It stretched across the globe faster than a stormy weather system. Some say our entire financial structure almost went over a cliff at that time. If that's not being connected, then what is? The world is smaller than ever, and this is a good thing. You can now be anyone from anywhere and make a difference. The opportunities are only limited to your thinking. But if you continue to wait for others to tell you what to believe and think, you limit your potential in the world. When you think for yourself, you tap into your own unique brilliance – a brilliance that can solve major problems from poverty to sickness. It's only your thinking that holds you back.

We Need Each Other

The power of connections is illustrated in Dr. Beth Chittick Nolan's story "The Eel and the Bartender" from the book *The*

Rhino with Glue-On Shoes and Other Surprising True Stories of Zoo Vets and Their Patients.[131] A moray eel is donated to the New England Aquarium by a bartender who had taken care of it for years in his bar. Dr. Nolan is called to help the eel because it refuses to eat and is quickly digressing. To her surprise, nothing seems to work until she calls the bartender for help. He is the only one that can coax the eel out of its hiding place, and he proceeds to feed it by hand. As Dr. Nolan writes, "I remember the look of pure adoration on the man's face as this eel emerged from its hiding place for him, and only him... their bond was even more elemental than the eel's hunger for food."

We all make these connections with others – especially with animals. This is no surprise if you have a pet you love in your life; you can relate to the deep bond that Dr. Nolan describes. The power of connections is as strong a need as food for all of us. When we don't have these connections from others, many times we turn to animals as a replacement. These connections feed us and help us discover a joyful life.

According to Daniel Gilbert, Harvard psychologist and best-selling author of *Stumbling on Happiness*, there is a secret to happiness: social connections. "We're one of the most social animals on our planet. We need each other for just about everything... when our social connections are strong, we're happy; when they're lost, we're devastated."[132]

Happiness Is Contagious

In Framingham, Massachusetts, in 1948 a study known as the Framingham Heart Study (FHS) began, studying the heart health of over 15,000 people. The social connections of the participants were studied over a thirty-two year period, and researchers calculated how changes in the happiness of any person affected the entire network. In other words, human happiness depends upon large clusters of people we don't even know. What the researchers found is that if your friend becomes happy, it increases your chance at happiness by 15 percent. Up to three degrees of separation changes the probability of impacting another's happiness. Happiness spreads through social networks like a virus – happiness is contagious.[133]

Using a mood scale completed at different exam points (as part of the FHS efforts to understand the relationship between depression and heart attacks), the researchers found a clear indication of happy and unhappy niches in the FHS social network. Like obesity and smoking, the spread of happiness among people was found to extend others. People who are surrounded by many happy people report being happier as time goes on. This finding supports the idea that happiness spreads with effects lasting up to a year.[134]

This study motivates us to follow the path of balance, joy, and peace, because we all tangibly benefit from it. We are inspired by knowing that our own self-development has palpable benefits for others, and it motivates us to keep going on this journey of discovery – because now it's not just about us.

The Power of the Heart

The heart is the most powerful part of the body. In the *The HeartMath Solution* by Doc Childre and Howard Martin, the authors share how scientists have begun to prove the power of the heart. They have discovered that "the heart's electromagnetic field is by far the most powerful produced by the body; it's approximately five thousand times greater in strength than the field produced by the brain... the heart's field not only permeates every cell in the body but also radiates outside of us and can be measured up to eight to ten feet away."[135]

They go on to say, "*HeartMath* demonstrates that when we focus attention on our hearts, the synchronization between our hearts and brains increases."[136] The energy that is contained in our heart's field isn't merely detected only by our own brains and bodies – it can also be registered by the people around us. If you want to learn more, we encourage you to read this book.

Community – A Unique Perspective

Scott Peck, the author of many self-development books (including *The Road Less Traveled* and *The Different Drum*), was a pioneer in building community. In the process, he came up with a list of characteristics that he believed made for true community. We agree with much of what Peck advocated and have added our own twists as well.

For a community to honor the diversity of all members and move forward with peaceful actions, the following components are required:

A Safe Container: All members must be allowed to speak from their heart. They must be able to be vulnerable and feel safe being so. They must be able to grow and change at their own pace.

Reflective and Aware: All members reflect on their motives as well as those of others in the community and the world around them. Awareness is actively encouraged. With reflection and awareness, we respond rather than react.

Diversity Is Encouraged: Every perspective is honored because it is needed to determine the best approach to any obstacles or tasks. When we embrace diversity and lean on consensus, the most innovative solution emerges. This is done by keeping the mind open and the heart engaged.

We Learn from Each Other: By relating with others we get a clear reflection of ourselves and see what doesn't work. We can choose to work on ourselves rather than requiring someone else to change.

Disagreements Are Normal: There will always be disagreements in a community. We encourage you to honor each person's perspective and find a path of agreement. This can include agreeing to disagree. Win-win solutions can be discovered by working with your own emotional state and being responsible for communicating in a productive and empowering manner.

Cooperative Leadership: Leadership is determined by the gifts and talents of each group member. The leader in any area will emerge because it is their talent and passion that guides and fits the harmonious flow of the whole.

Community Spirit: The true spirit of community is the spirit of peace, love, wisdom, and power. We work and play together.

Once community is established, we begin supporting each other with our natural strengths. This enables us to step in effortlessly when help is needed. You don't always have to pay somebody to do things for you. It's not about trying to save anybody. Loving effortlessly becomes an action, not just a feeling.

Diversity Is Strength in All Communities

When individuals are allowed to express their own unique perspectives, they find others of like interests. This diversity creates strength within a community that provides diverse offerings from those who have discovered their passion. If you're not allowed to express your perspective, you won't be able to discover your passion. Diversity is the nature of creation. As Deepak Chopra says, "The Universe is set up for maximum diversity."[137] See your internal self as the microcosm of life and your community as the macrocosm. Our bodies are an intricate and interrelated system. The digestive, respiratory, circulatory, musculoskeletal, and nervous systems all work in balance and harmony. No one system is more important than the other. This harmonious diversity keeps us alive, strong, and able to adapt to numerous environments and situations. When you can accept the diversity within the microcosm that is you, with all of your emotional facets, then you can accept the diversity in your outer community. You have more to offer, more opportunities to allow facets of yourself (known or unknown) to connect with others. "Our human potential is to recognize how much harmony we truly are together," is how Maya Angelou expresses it.[138]

The uniqueness of our individuality helps us to create in ways that help us all evolve and improves all of our lives (the Internet, computers, cell phones, etc.). What makes us similar is the continuity and well-being that gives us stability. It's the need for continuity and the creative individual brilliance that makes our world an increasingly better place to live. It's the best of collaboration in ways we don't see. As Herbie Hancock says, "I believe human beings have the capacity to find various viewpoints to approach a problem or to find a solution. There are an infinite number of ways to look at things, or to hear them."[139]

Community Tames Your Ego

Community is the source for collective genius. You have the opportunity to see outside of yourself as well as see the diversity from within. You witness a different way of handling something, and it becomes a teachable point – just like watching movies.

The ego is about ensuring that one's individualism is preserved and protected. It has a tendency to get distorted and become self-focused to the extent that it's difficult to see and understand outside of it. Being in community is the practice of releasing the ego and connecting with the whole. The ego wants to retain its individualism; community is about retaining and sustaining each other. The more we gravitate towards community, the more aware we are of our ego and the better opportunity we have to soften it, accept it, and keep it in its place. A community gives us constant opportunities for this awareness. As a result, we all get a chance to grow and create a better way of living together. As Maya Angelou says, "The ego binds, love liberates."[140] In community we get to practice loving.

"My Way," made famous by Frank Sinatra, and "I Am Woman" by Helen Reddy are two songs frequently used at funerals because they represent how people have lived their lives. The male anthem is usually the former and the female version the latter. While we all can relate to the empowering aspects of these popular songs, they have mixed meanings and outcomes for our lives. Doing things "my" way or "roaring" through life may bring short-term satisfaction, but can this resonate for an entire life? Many times, this approach ends up causing more harm to others and provides little upside for us. Additionally, force always requires more energy, which makes this approach feel like an uphill journey.

Both songs focus on the individuality of doing life on your own. While it's good to come from these places of empowerment, they don't always bring us the lasting peace and joy we all desire. Neither song talks about how others assist us to achieve what we have accomplished. Success in life is rarely achieved without help from others.

We're not saying you shouldn't live your life your way or without gusto. Do it your way, but do it with love. Your default becomes a choice for love instead of emotional, hard-charging reactions. When you look back at your life, you'll also be grateful for the connections this loving way of living created for you and the success your influence had on others.

Create Community Within

Establishing a community of emotions within allows community engagement with others in your outer life. The feeling of being home is found within community. We have to be at home within our own emotions before we're ready for others. Recognizing our emotions prepares us for this joyful way of living.

If your family belief system is your reference point in all situations, it becomes a barrier to community and creates a wall that contains you and keeps community out. When you're respectful and honor all perspectives and traditions, you bring down the wall and connect with something entirely new. "When I learn to meet my thinking as a friend, I notice I can meet every human as a friend."[141]

How Do You Make Meaningful Connections with Others?

"Weeds are flowers too, once you get to know them."
— A.A. Milne, creator of Winnie the Pooh (via Eeyore)

Taking risks, meeting of the minds, and heart connections with others can be awkward, slow, scary, and just plain weird. There's a natural unfolding that happens in all relationships, be it romantic or not. Look for things you like in another person, and make that your focus. Try not to see others' differences as invalid; instead, embrace them and see where they take you.

Breaking Bread with One Another

A good place to build connections is to start by breaking bread — eating a meal together with the people in your life. There's no better place to begin than with your own family. In this fast-paced world of ours, it's easy to lose touch with the art of celebrating life and each other over a delicious and carefully prepared meal. We're all such accomplished time-maximizers that we rarely slow down to have a meal together. It just doesn't seem efficient, when you can grab something on the run to the next task or do what has become a common workplace practice — eat at your desk.

When you take time to share a meal together, everything is lighter and easier. People relax, enjoy the food, and for a few brief moments, they slow down and forget the next task at hand. In these moments, we start to connect with each other. For families, a daily meal together helps to keep a family connected, and parents are able to get a sense of how the children are doing. There's much research on the benefits of families eating dinner together and how it impacts their lives. In cultures throughout Europe, people continue to foster the tradition of preparing long meals and dining together leisurely.

Breaking bread together also fosters stronger relationships in the community and the workplace. When you find yourself in a stalemate with someone at work, a client, a neighbor, or anyone in your life, and you can't seem to move forward with that person, try breaking bread with him or her. Watch how the issues are easier to discuss, how looking at each other in a calm, off-site environment makes it easier to understand the other person's perspective – or at least hear it. This is especially true in today's companies. They are moving so fast and trying to adjust to our rapidly changing times that people can get pushed aside. Look at the derivation for the word "company." It comes from the Old French *compainie* and is related to *compaignon*. When you look at the origin of the Old French, it literally translates as "one who breaks bread with another." It's also based on the Latin *com* (together with) plus *panis* (bread).

Jesus gave us only one commandment: to love your neighbor as yourself. He then proceeded to show us how to do it by the way he lived. We believe the Last Supper was one of the ways he showed us. When Jesus asked us to "do this in memory of me," he was giving us another example of how to love by breaking bread together.

Expand Your Family Circle

We all know the inherent value of close family connections. These connections are strong, traditions are formed, and love grows. Many times, we become overprotective about whom we call family, and anyone not in the club is excluded. This commonly plays out when a family member marries. Other family members sometime exclude the new spouse because he or she is not "family."

This person (or anyone else that's new) is not to be trusted and is effectively kept outside of the familial circle. He or she can only get in once trust is certain, and even then risks being exiled. As Jack Byrnes (Robert De Niro) says to his new son-in-law (Ben Stiller) in *Meet the Parents*,[142] "See, if I can't trust you Greg, then I'll have no choice but to put you right back outside the circle, and once you're out, you're out – there's no coming back."

Jack Byrnes' approach *is* funny, and it's not far from what we unconsciously do to others outside of our recognized family boundaries. We are taught to believe that this level of trust isn't possible outside of our family. As Jack explains to Greg, "Let me ask you a question, Greg. Let's just say you have kids... and you wanna get out of the house, spend a night on the town. So, you hire a babysitter, someone you think you can trust. References, work experience – it all checks out fine. But then how do you really know for certain... that your loved ones are safe with this stranger? I mean, can you ever really trust another human being, Greg? No. The answer is, you cannot."

To realize the full benefits of community, be willing to believe and trust in others. It's ironic how we cling to our own family's circle of trust, yet most of us don't live with each other year-round. If we expanded our concept of family, we could connect with our neighbors and community in ways that would be equally fulfilling. We live on top of each other and still have no proximity. Online communities just show us what individuals want us to see; we don't see how they behave in their everyday life. We try to avoid allowing people to see our foibles, yet sometimes these qualities can be the most interesting sides of us and we don't even know it. Be willing to accept others as they are, and in turn be real about who you are, too. You may just find a new expansion to your family that will bring you joy.

The movie *Feast of Love*[143] is an example of how our lives converge. Life is so much sweeter when we accept, help, tolerate, and love each other. Each of us gets through our struggles and the lessons of life easier when we have more than just a genetic family, but also a family of others who are there for us. This movie shows us how supportive a diverse community can be in our lives. Sometimes others in our community can reach us in ways our mates and family can't. When we open our hearts to others, we can heal faster and find the tangible connections we all desire.

One of the characters, Chloe Barlow, knows her spouse is going to die, but she focuses her passion for him, staying motivated in hope and love. She doesn't give up and fully enjoys her time with him until he passes. Because she has bonded with others in her community, she receives love and support in beautiful ways.

It's the rain *and* the sun that makes a rainbow, just as both pain and joy make life beautiful. This illustrates the duality of life. It's not that it's joy *or* pain – it's the continuum of joy and its lack (what we call pain). Rain without the sun doesn't make a rainbow. You need both ingredients before you can see the rainbow. It's the same with pain and joy – both are necessary in order to recognize the beauty of life. Think of it as Maya Angelou says: "I don't ever feel I have no help. I've had rainbows in my clouds and the thing to do, it seems to me, is to prepare yourself so that you can be a rainbow in somebody else's cloud... be a blessing to somebody."[144]

> *"We are to hold each other and to let each other go. One movement makes possible the other. Distance gives the space in which to reach out and hold. The intimacy of holding gives strength to the inner person – the nourishment that enables us to speed another on his way. To stand on one's own two feet may be the real work of love."*
> *– Elizabeth O'Connor*

Living Life with Sustained Joy

Too often, we live our lives immersed in illusions that we think will lead us to sustained joy. If we just had the right home, the right spouse, the right job, healthy children, numerous friends, and financial freedom, then we would be happy. It's only through a diverse life where joy can be sustained. You may get the right job, but if that's all you have, one day, for numerous reasons, it will not be able to provide the joy you seek. Life will always be an experience of constant change. When you embrace this truth, life doesn't have to always be about your external image of what success looks like.

How Do You Live Life This Way?

❖ Go with the flow of life – don't push against what is.

❖ Think for yourself and trust your instincts.

❖ See the big picture.

❖ Let go and allow.

❖ Use the Emotional Circle of Life as a compass to discover where you are on your journey and what to focus on.

❖ Draw on any resource in the sphere of your being to enable you to stay relaxed and alert, peaceful, and ready.

❖ Make your passion freedom and your purpose love. 🔳

✖ CHAPTER SUMMARY ✖

"Nothing is either good or bad but thinking makes it so."
– William Shakespeare

Whatever path you're on, you're moving towards a place of openness and love, a feeling of being home. There is no one right path. We each have a unique journey, with desires that aren't exactly the same for any two people. Whichever country, religion, politics, or culture you come from, they all can lead you home. Ideally, home is a place of acceptance, openness, tolerance, love, and peace of mind. To have that, you have to be okay with all of your emotions. Otherwise, you'll get yourself stuck in emotional grooves, you'll identify with your emotions as the truthful you, and then you'll act accordingly. This isn't wrong or bad – it just lengthens the journey home. As you put into practice what you've learned in this book, you'll gain more clarity on how each lesson applies uniquely to you.

BELIEF STATEMENTS REPRESENTED IN THIS CHAPTER:

Energizing Beliefs

❖ I am immune to gossip.

❖ Love is the only truth.

❖ I resolve confusion in all relationships.

❖ The only thing permanent is change.

❖ Great change is the road to transformation.

❖ I accept the changes occurring in my life.

❖ Each day I forgive myself more and more.

❖ I take risks and try new things to see how they feel.

❖ Critics are paid to critique, and that's okay with me — that's what they do.

❖ I'm more confident in my relationships.

❖ It's my journey with others that makes my life a delight and worth living.

❖ I find ways to allow my heart to lead.

❖ The journey of life is better with company.

❖ When I'm in community, I speak from my heart.

❖ I'm open to asking for advice and receiving it.

De-Energizing Beliefs

❖ I jump to conclusions and assume the worst.

❖ I'm a chameleon; I change myself for others in the name of love.

❖ I have to try and make this marriage work.

❖ If I could end my marriage, I'd be happy and free.

❖ If I could just move, I'd be happy.

❖ I run away from all the great possibilities of my life.

❖ I'm bankrupt in my finances, my relationships, and how I feel about myself.

❖ I'm afraid of taking the first step because it seems so dangerous.

❖ My life is about always trying to get somewhere other than where I am now.

❖ I keep moving down the road I chose in the past.

❖ I think that because I have money I am all-powerful.

❖ I don't have time to connect to others; it's all about doing and accomplishing the next goal.

❖ My life underwhelms me.

❖ I can't see a way to conduct business that puts people first.

❖ I find it hard to love people.

❖ I keep wanting my loved ones to be someone or something they're not.

❖ My future prospects are uninspiring.

❖ I can't let go because the details always get screwed up.

❖ I bury the pain because it just hurts too much.

MUSIC SELECTIONS

"Ease on Down the Road," Michael Jackson

"Sweet Emotion," Aerosmith

"Real Emotions," Los Lonely Boys

"C'mon C'mon," Sheryl Crow

"Just Show Me How," Sarah Brightman

ESSENTIAL OIL RECOMMENDATIONS

Elemi - Its fragrance is very conducive towards meditation.

Myrtle - Supports the respiratory system. It has been researched for its effects on glandular imbalances and its soothing effects when inhaled. Its fragrance influence is elevating and euphoric.

Citrus Fresh - A relaxing, calming blend loved by children and adults alike. It supports the immune system and overall health while bringing about a sense of well-being, creativity, and joy. Improves mental accuracy and concentration; it also works as an air purifier.

Gratitude - A soothing blend designed to elevate the spirit, calm the emotions, and bring relief to the body, while helping to foster a grateful attitude.

Sensation - A wonderfully fragrant, powerfully romantic blend that is extremely uplifting and refreshing. It amplifies excitement, self-expression, and awareness. It was formulated to enhance the enjoyment of special moments.

Final Thoughts

We don't have all the answers, nor do we purport this work as a panacea. We can only give you our experience as to what you might expect. See your process with this book as a lifestyle change, a new way of living. Here are some of the lifestyle changes we noticed while writing this book.

We became more aware of the seasonality of our emotions. We continue to get better and better at accepting them as passing and not permanent. We began to trust our emotions as a powerful compass, and we were able to recognize when we were off track. Some days were better than others, and the better ones started to outnumber the unpleasant days. Other people's emotional experiences don't seem to rattle us as they did in the past. As a result, we have become better listeners, we judge less, and we've found a different way to experience compassion. It wasn't until we could allow compassion for ourselves that we could be there for others.

Peace of mind started to visit us in the most delightful ways. There was less of an internal struggle, and our reactivity was reduced. A type of balance set in that was similar to riding a bike. The more we practice, the less effort it takes. When we fall down – and we do! – we just get back on the bicycle and rediscover our balance.

We don't get so scared by our emotions and that of others as we did in the past. There's a growing acceptance that's liberating.

Others can see the changes in us. Some are not sure what they see, and others tell us, "I want what you have." Additionally, it's easier to connect with people – both those we know and those we don't. It truly has become a joy to meet new people and form new friendships.

Just like any other lifestyle change, it's best to take it one step at a time. If you've ever set out to improve your health, did you try to do it all at once by changing your diet and running a marathon the next week? At times, we pushed it too much and didn't follow our own natural pace. Remember, when you're diving for pearls, you can go too deep at times, making it difficult to surface, so take your time. Determine which emotion or chapter you want to focus on and take baby steps. Perhaps you might enjoy forming your own team to assist with the process. Watching movies with others is a delightful way to flow with this book. It's how we did it, and by coming together, we bonded in ways we didn't expect. Additionally, friends help motivate us to keep going and overcome the obstacles that may appear along the way.

Most importantly, be gentle with yourself. This lifestyle change isn't about "making it happen." It's about discovering peace and experiencing more joy in your life.

MOVIE LIST

Chapter 5

Chapter 6

ABOUT THE AUTHORS

SUE-ANNE MacGREGOR

For as long as Sue-Anne MacGregor can remember, she has felt a spiritual connection that has inspired her to help others. Holistic medicine and healing techniques appealed to her at an early age, and throughout a sixteen-year career with IBM, in which she served as an account manager and trainer in the United States, Hong Kong, Japan, and Australia.

She was born in Sydney, Australia, where Sue-Anne lived until moving to the US in 1988. Facing adversity in her own life, Sue-Anne discovered complementary therapies that guided her process of healing. She undertook extensive training in both Australia and the US in the areas of meditation, the alternative healing practice of Reiki, inner child therapy, flower essences, nutrition, essential oils, transformational touch, and Resonance Repatterning. Sue-Anne is a minister and has the highly refined intuitive abilities of clairvoyance, clairsentience, and clairaudience.

Since 1999 Sue-Anne has utilized her experience and abilities to coach CEOs, families, couples, and individuals. She assists them in aligning with their most positive, peaceful beliefs, and working with their emotions so they can reach their full potential.

Sue-Anne MacGregor co-founded *Peace Of Mind Overtures* with David Barnes and together they have co-authored two books on human emotional patterns that are soon to be released. She lives in Allen, TX with her husband, Dr. Tom Lenahan and their cat OC.

DAVID BARNES

David Barnes was born in Cleveland, Ohio and has been a life-long student of self-development and inspirational thinking. After graduating from The Ohio State University, he went to work for the Ford Motor Company. His diverse background in marketing, sales, and corporate finance put him on an executive leadership path with Ford. After ten years with the company and extensive geographical moves, David left Ford to take an executive position as Vice President of Marketing and Communications with the Dallas Symphony Orchestra. There he directed all aspects of sales, marketing, branding, and public relations for the orchestra.

David left the symphony to embark on his own consulting and to deepen his knowledge and self-development, looking for accessible ways to implement these ideas in the workplace. During this period of discovery, he studied modern and historic works of the great teachers in leadership, business, inspirational thinking, and spirituality from all traditions.

David co-founded *Peace Of Mind Overtures* with Sue-Anne MacGregor. Together, they are building a firm dedicated to providing pathways to peace of mind for individuals, families, and businesses. He currently lives in Plano, TX with his wife Lura and their children Sarah, Michael and dog Murphy.

Endnotes

1   Renee Zellweger, *Iconoclasts,* Season 1, Episode 3: Renee Zellweger on Christiane Amanpour.

2   Sting, "The Yoga Behind the Music," *Energy Times,* October, 2010, p.25.

3   Elizabeth Anne Jones, Candace Pert, *Awaken to Healing Fragrance: The Power of Essential Oil Therapy,* (Berkeley, CA: North Atlantic Books, 2010).

4   Daniel Goleman, *Emotional Intelligence* (New York: Bantam, 2006).

5   Stephen Herek, *Life or Something Like It,* 2002.

6   Gus Van Sant, *Finding Forrester,* 2000.

7   David Brooks, *The New York Times,* "The Empathy Issue," May 29, 2009.

8   Eckhart Tolle, *The Power of Now* (Novato, CA: New World Library, 2004).

9   Oprah Winfrey Show, May 17, 2010.

10 *Iconoclasts,* Season 4, Episode 3: Tony Hawk and John Favreau.

11 All essential oil recommendations have been taken from *Essential Oils Desk Reference,* Fourth Edition, compiled by Essential Science Publishing, 2007.

12 Diane English, *The Women,* 2008.

13 Byron Katie, *Loving What Is* (New York: Three Rivers Press, 2003).

14 Jack Kornfield, *After the Ecstasy, the Laundry* (NY: Bantam, 2001).

15 Byron Katie, *Loving What Is,* (New York: Three Rivers Press, 2003).

16 Giuseppe Tornatore, *The Legend of 1900,* 1998.

17 Woody Allen, *Vicki Cristina Barcelona,* 2008.

18 Scott Cooper, *Crazy Heart,* 2009.

19 Dr. Christiane Northrup, *Women's Bodies, Women's Wisdom,* PBS, 2010.

20 *Iconoclasts,* Season 2, Episode 6: Dave Chappelle and Maya Angelou.

21 James L. Brooks, *As Good as It Gets,* 1997.

22 Samuel Baum, *Lie to Me,* Fox, 2009.

23 Gavin De Becker, *The Gift of Fear* (New York: Dell, 1998).

24 Noah Baumbach, *The Squid and the Whale,* 2009.

25 Carl Orff, *Carmine Burana,* 1935.

26 Dr. Martin Luther King, Jr., *A Testament to Hope* (New York: HarperOne, 1990).

27 Tom Hooper, *The King's Speech,* 2010.

28 Mirabai Starr, *St. Francis of Assisi* (Louisville, CO: Sounds True, Inc., 2007).

29 Nick Cassavetes, *My Sister's Keeper,* 2009.

30 Sri Mata Amritanandamayi Devi (Amma), *From Amma's Heart*, 2003.

31 Todd Haynes, *Far from Heaven*, 2002.

32 Tom Ford, *A Single Man*, 2009.

33 Tom Shadyac, *Liar, Liar*, 2007.

34 Chris Weitz, *Down to Earth*, 2001.

35 Peter Jackson, *The Lord of the Rings: Fellowship of the Ring*, 2001.

36 *Iconoclasts*, Season 5, Episode 3: Hugh Jackman and Jean-Georges Vongerichten.

37 Ibid.

38 Ibid.

39 Ibid.

40 Randall Miller, *Bottle Shock*, 2008.

41 Norah Ephron, *Julie & Julia*, 2009.

42 Mark Rydell, *On Golden Pond*, 1981.

43 Barry Sonnenfeld, *RV*, 2006.

44 CBS, *60 Minutes*, Lady Gaga, February 13, 2011.

45 Byron Katie, *Loving What Is* (Louisville, CO: Three Rivers Press, 2003).

46 Aaron Schneider, *Get Low*, 2009.

47 Dr. Kristen Neff, quoted in an article by Tara Parker-Pope in *The New York Times*, February 28, 2011.

48 *Iconoclasts*, Season 2, Episode 6: Dave Chappelle and Maya Angelou.

49 Doug Liman, *Fair Game*, 2010.

50 Brian Gibson, *The Josephine Baker Story*, 1991.

51 Byron Katie, *Loving What Is* (Louisville, CO: Three Rivers Press, 2003).

52 Ken Kwapis, *License to Wed*, 2007.

53 Ron Howard, *Cinderella Man*, 2005.

54 http://en.wikipedia.org/wiki/Reinhold_Niebuhr.

55 Patanjali's *Yoga Sutras*, 2.16.

56 *The Oprah Winfrey Show*, "Dr. Oz Holds an Intervention," September 29, 2009.

57 Kirk Jones, *Everybody's Fine*, 2009.

58 Susan Bier, *After the Wedding*, 2006.

59 Fowler, Earlene, *Kansas Troubles* (New York: Berkeley Books, 1997).

60 Tyler Perry, *Why Did I Get Married?*, 2007.

61 Brian Koppelman, David Levien, *Solitary Man*, 2009.

62 Guillermo Arriaga, *The Burning Plain*, 2008.

63   Roger Michell, *Notting Hill*, 1999.

64   Vincent Ward, *What Dreams May Come*, 1998.

65   Frederik Du Chau, *Quest for Camelot*, 1998.

66   Stanley Kubrick, *Eyes Wide Shut*, 1999.

67   Francois Girard, *The Red Violin*, 1998.

68   Frank B. Goodin II, *Love Trap*, 2005.

69   Irwin Winkler, *De-Lovely*, 2004.

70   Adrian Lyne, *Unfaithful*, 2002.

71   Stanley Kubrick, *Eyes Wide Shut*, 1999.

72   David Schnarch, PhD, *Passionate Marriage* (New York: W.W.Norton & Co., 2009).

73   Paul Thomas Anderson, *There Will Be Blood*, 2007.

74   Walter Hill, *Brewter's Millions,*1985.

75   Stephen R. Covey, *The 7 Habits of Highly Effective Families* (New York: St. Martin's Griffin, 1997).

76   Tony Scott, *Unstoppable*, 2010.

77   Ron Underwood, *City Slickers*, 1991.

78   Ethan and Joel Coen, *A Serious Man*, 2009.

79   Gabriel Axel, *Babette's Feast*, 1987.

80   Ricky Gervais, Matthew Robinson, *The Invention of Lying*, 2009.

81   Robert Luketic, *The Ugly Truth*, 2009.

82   Peyton Reed, *Yes Man*, 2008.

83   Doug Bollinger, Bx Giongrete, *Waltzing Anna*, 2006.

84   Kathryn Bigelow, *The Hurt Locker*, 2008.

85   Frank Coraci, *The Waterboy*, 1998.

86   Frederik Du Chau, *Quest for Camelot*, 1998.

87   Peter Cattaneo, *The Rocker*, 2008.

88   Wes Anderson, *The Fantastic Mr. Fox*, 2009.

89   James Burrows, Les and Glen Charles, *Cheers*, 1992-1983.

90   Anne Fletcher, *The Proposal*, 2009.

91   Ridley Scott, *A Good Year*, 2006.

92   Woody Allen, *Whatever Works*, 2009.

93   Jimmy Page, quoted in *It Might Get Loud*, Davis Guggenheim, 2009.

94   Roland Joffé, *The Mission*, 1986.

95   Frederik Du Chau, *Quest for Camelot*, 1998.

96   Kevin Lima, *Enchanted,* 1998.

97   "An Evolve-By Date," *New York Times,* November 24, 2009.

98   *Iconoclasts,* Season 2, Episode 6, Dave Chapelle and Maya Angelou.

99   Clint Eastwood, *Hereafter,* 2010.

100 Wayne Wang, *The Last Holiday,* 2006.

101 Isabel Coixet, *Elegy,* 2008.

102 Mike Nichols, *The Birdcage,* 1996.

103 Darren Aronofsky, *The Black Swan,* 2010.

104 *Iconoclasts,* Season 5, Episode 3: Hugh Jackman and Jean-Georges Vongerichten.

105 Ibid.

106 Dan Buettner, *The Blue Zones: Lessons for Living Longer from People Who've Lived the Longest* (Washington, DC: National Geographic, 2010).

107 Ivan Reitman, *Dave,* 1993.

108 Sri Mata Amritanandamayi (Amma), *From Amma's Heart,* Translated and Written by Swami Amritaswarupananda, Mata Amritanandamayi Mission Trust.

109 D. Max Moerman quote, Barnard College.

110 Jon Poll, *Charlie Bartlett,* 2007.

111 John Lee Hancock, *The Blind Side,* 2009.

112 *Iconoclasts,* Sundance Channel, Season 2, Episode 6: Dave Chapelle and Maya Angelou.

113 Mike Barker, *A Good Woman,* 2004.

114 *Status Anxiety* (unabridged), Alain de Botton, Blackstone Audio, Inc, 2006.

115 Ryan Murphy, *Eat Pray Love,* 2010.

116 *Iconoclasts,* Season 4, Episode 1: Desmond Tutu and Richard Branson.

117 Alain de Botton, "A Kinder, Gentler Philosophy of Success," Ted Talks, July 2009.

118 Ibid.

119 Sidney Pollack, *Sketches of Frank Gehry,* 2005.

120 *Iconoclasts,* Season 2, Episode 3: Quentin Tarantino and Fiona Apple.

121 Ibid.

122 Dean DeBlois, Chris Sanders, *How to Train Your Dragon,* 2010.

123 Raymond De Felitta, *City Island,* 2010.

124 Kay Pollak, *As It Is in Heaven,* 2004.

125 Sidney Lumet, *The Wiz*, 1978.

126 http://www.bosu.com/scripts/cgiip.exe/WService=BOSU/story.html?article=4452.

127 *Iconoclasts*, Season 3, Episode 3: Mike Myers and Deepak Chopra.

128 Jason Reitman, *Up in the Air*, 2009.

129 Richard Ledes, *The Caller*, 2008.

130 *Iconoclasts*, Season 4, Episode 1: Desmond Tutu and Richard Branson.

131 Lucy Spelman and Ted Y. Mashima, *The Rhino with Glue-On Shoes: And Other Surprising True Stories of Zoo Vets and Their Patients* (New York: Delacorte Press, 2008).

132 "Rethinking Happiness," *This Emotional Life*, PBS.

133 Daniel Gilbert, "Rethinking Happiness," This Emotional Life, PBS.

134 See Framingham Heart Study. Also, *This Emotional Life Series:* "Rethinking Happiness," PBS.

135 Doc Childre and Howard Martin, *The HeartMath Solution* (New York: HarperOne, 2000), p. 33.

136 Ibid. p.34.

137 *Iconoclasts*, Season 4, Episode 4: Mike Myers and Deepak Chopra.

138 *Iconoclasts*, Season 2, Episode 2: Dave Chappell and Maya Angelou.

139 Herbie Hancock, *Wall Street Journal*, June 22, 2010.

140 *Oprah Winfrey Presents Master Class:* Maya Angelou, January 26, 2011.

141 Byron Katie with Stephen Mitchell, *Loving What Is: Four Questions That Can Change Your Life* (Audio Literature, 2002).

142 Jay Roach, *Meet the Parents*, 2000.

143 Robert Benton, *Feast of Love*, 2007.

144 *Oprah Winfrey Presents Master Class:* Maya Angelou, January 26, 2011

CPSIA information can be obtained
at www.ICGtesting.com
Printed in the USA
FSOW02n2146020215
4922FS